A Guide to Library Sources in Political Science: American Government

Clement E. Vose
Wesleyan University

American Political Science Association
1527 New Hampshire Avenue, N.W.
Washington, D.C. 20036

The preparation of *A Guide to Library Sources in Political Science: American Government* was supported by Grant GY 9351 from the National Science Foundation to the American Political Science Association for a project to improve undergraduate education in political science. Sheilah R. Koeppen, Associate Director of the Division of Educational Affairs is the project director. Responsibility to the profession for project activities, 1972-1975, is exercised by this Steering Committee on Undergraduate Education:

    Vernon Van Dyke, Chairman, University of Iowa
    Vincent J. Browne, Jr., Howard University
    Gloria Carrig, Loop College, City Colleges of Chicago
    Martin Diamond, Northern Illinois University
    Heinz Eulau, Stanford University
    Betty Nesvold, California State University-San Diego
    Jack Peltason, Chancellor, University of Illinois
    Ithiel deS. Pool, Massachusetts Institute of Technology
    James A. Robinson, President, University of West Florida
    Stanley Rothman, Smith College

This monograph has been commissioned by the Steering Committee on Undergraduate Education. It has been reviewed by three qualified persons, including two members of the Steering Committee. The monograph is published under the auspices of the Division of Educational Affairs. However, the views expressed are those of the author and not of the Steering Committee or of the American Political Science Association.

©1975 by The American Political Science Association, 1527 New Hampshire Avenue, Washington, D.C. 20036, under International and Pan-American Copyright Conventions. All rights reserved. No part of this book may be reproduced in any form or by any means without permission in writing from the publisher. Printed in the United States of America. ISBN O-915654-03-2

Contents

Foreword by Evron M. Kirkpatrick v
Preface vii

PART ONE: AMERICAN NATIONAL GOVERNMENT 1
1. Government Publications 3
2. The Constitution 9
3. Congress 13
4. The Executive Branch 33
5. Federal Courts 43

PART TWO: GENERAL REFERENCE BOOKS 51
6. Almanacs 53
7. Biographies 57
8. Political Dictionaries 69
9. Encyclopedias 87

PART THREE: THE POLITICAL SCIENTIST IN THE LIBRARY . . 99
10. Library Basics 101
11. Files, Archives and Manuscripts 123

Foreword

Among the major activities of the American Political Science Association, the publication of the *American Political Science Review* and the Annual Meeting provide for exchange of information about research. Other major activities aim to adapt research to teaching needs, particularly at the undergraduate level.

Since the Association's establishment in 1904, there has always been a committee concerned with undergraduate education and, in each decade, an education committee has issued a report recommending instructional goals and strategies. Today, we have a different concept of useful educational activity; the Association is helping prepare instructional materials that can be utilized by teachers and students. The regional seminars for college teachers in the 1960s, supported by a grant from the Ford Foundation, were a notable first effort of this sort. The seminars helped teachers locate and use new sources of course materials and different methods of instruction. Several hundred political scientists participated in these seminars.

At the end of 1972, with the support of a grant from the National Science Foundation, the Association established a Division of Educational Affairs and began to develop publications providing teachers and students with instructional guides and useful materials. *DEA NEWS for Teachers of Political Science*, a newspaper received by all Association members; SETUPS, that are student learning materials prepared by faculty in a workshop hosted by the Inter-University Consortium for Political Research; and a Bulletin for undergraduates on *Careers and the Study of Political Science* are the initial publications.

This volume, *A Guide to Library Sources in Political Science: American Government*, is the first in a series of Monographs for Teachers of Political Science. The Guide helps satisfy the many requests we receive from teachers and librarians for information about documentary and reference sources for political science. Its merit is due to Clement E. Vose's knowledge of the subject and to his enthusiasm and wit in writing about it. Professor Vose long has sought to share his expertise with teachers and students and to facilitate the growth and organization of library and archival collections. He has contributed critical essays on documentary and reference sources to our professional journals and encyclopedias, and he currently serves as the Association's representative on the National Archives Advisory Council. Additionally, one of the most useful and popular offerings in the Association's regional seminar program was the seminar he conducted on the topic of library collections for political science.

It is a great pleasure to initiate a series of educational publications with *A Guide to Library Sources in Political Science: American Government* and I look forward to further monographs that will be of value to teachers of political science.

Evron M. Kirkpatrick
Executive Director
American Political Science Association
January, 1975

Preface

The aim in these essays about how political scientists, young and old, might garner knowledge from libraries is to catch the reader's interest as a spur to further individual study. The try is to catch and stimulate curiosity, not to satiate it.

By examining the way in which certain topics and institutions are documented, it is expected that readers will be enabled to look afresh at many other matters not spoken of here. State governments in the United States, for example, are patterned after national institutions and so is much of the documentation. A person who understands the relationship of the *United States Code* to Federal statutes will find identical patterns of publishing the laws enacted by state legislatures. Judicial reports are also similar. For this reason there is no independent treatment of state politics and government.

The libraries of the world exist to be explored by individuals. Try an afternoon, or even half an hour, comparing how dictionaries deal with a single political word; how atlases locate Alaska and Hawaii in relation to the other 48 states; how encyclopedias compare one to the other. A speed test in the library is likely to be won by people who have spent much idleness reading and pondering. It is hoped that an examination of this monograph will help. It cannot promise to help those who do not help themselves. The trick to be accomplished is to master and remaster the library, not to memorize the poor precepts of this introduction to the topic. Good luck.

There are so few occasions when one can acknowledge unpayable debts to friends whose influence and help came long ago, but it is so keenly felt that a chance like this must be grasped. Oliver Garceau first gave me a serious library research assignment—on the white primary, at the University of Maine. By example and through his kindnesses, David Fellman taught me how to scamper efficiently around the law library at the University of Wisconsin. Ivan Stone, at Beloit College, encouraged me to teach undergraduates about the library in as systematic a way as I knew how in 1952. There I used *A Guide to the Study of Public Affairs* by E.E.

Schattschneider, Victor Jones and Stephen K. Bailey which had just been published. Later, for some dozen years until his death in 1971, I benefited from a warm colleagueship with Professor Schattschneider and delved deeper into sources of information in libraries.

For several years at Wesleyan I have taught a short course called "The Library in Political Studies" in concert with two superbly informed and congenial reference librarians, Joan Jurale and Edmund Rubacha. We have been assisted directly by undergraduate teaching apprentices, Samuel F. Saracino and Cathryn Connolly. Other Wesleyan students including Rebecca Vose were helpful. In preparing this introduction to libraries I was able to engage Samuel F. Saracino as a research assistant, much to my benefit. Although the work has been checked and double-checked by my secretary, Mrs. Mildred Pugh, it is very likely that I have managed to slip in some errors—for which I take full responsibility.

Some passages in this guide are drawn from other writings by me, perhaps verbatim but usually changed to suit immediate purposes. Thus there may be occasional resemblances to my article, "Reference Materials" in the *International Encyclopedia of the Social Science* and to my article "Library Reference Materials and Manuscripts as Data for Political Science" written some time ago for *The Handbook of Political Science,* now scheduled for publication in 1975. The section on political dictionaries is drawn almost wholly from my article "Political Dictionaries: A Bibliographical Essay" in the *American Political Science Review,* December, 1974. Part of Chapter 10 was published in the *Microform Review.*

Finally, I am grateful for the initiative of Sheilah Koeppen in launching me on this particular study and to Stephen McCarthy, Jack Peltason and Stanley Rothman for their suggestions and support. My Wesleyan colleague Russell D. Murphy has also helped me in numerous ways. Typing assistance was also provided by Mrs. Rhonda Kissinger and Mrs. Lee Messina. I received considerable aid and guidance from Quentin Riegel and William R. Van Saun.

Most photographs are owned outright by me. Credits include the following: Riegel, pp. 5, 10, 14, 18, 19, 27, 39, 55, 64, 72, 104, 112, 126 and 129; Nickens, p. 103; and Worldwide, p. 125.

Clement E. Vose
Middletown, Connecticut
March 18, 1975

Part One: American National Government

1. Government Publications

The publication and dissemination of reference materials by governments—local, regional, national and international—is a remarkable development in the whole conception of government, which has, at the same time, amply fed the hunger for knowledge about society. In England there was a long battle over the right of government to keep its processes secret, and, at first, reporting of the debates of Parliament was guarded. Great initiative and courage were needed in the development of a commercial system of publishing the proceedings of Parliament. This pattern has been followed in most democratic nations. Executive, or secret, sessions of the U.S. Senate declined markedly when members were popularly elected after 1913, for example. Legislative reports, the orders of administrative agencies, and the decisions of courts were once kept so private by government that commercial printers, and later large corporate publishers, grasped the opportunity to sell the available information to the public. In democratic countries a claim of the public's right to know coincided with the development of bureaucracies that were willing and able to offer the same information through government printing facilities. Thus, in the United States the Government Printing Office was formed in 1861. It took over the publication of reports of Supreme Court cases from private hands in 1872 and also the debates of the national legislature with the initiation of the *Congressional Record* the following year. Even today the official reports of cases in the lower Federal courts are published by the West Publishing Company, not the G.P.O.

Congress had been gradually developing a principle of public information in the publication of its laws, its debates, and its reports prior to the Civil War. The Government Printing Office was established within the legislative branch of the government and is supervised by the Joint Committee on Printing. While its head, the Public Printer, is appointed by the President with the advice and consent of the Senate, the G.P.O. is really run by Congress. Yet the Government Printing Office serves the entire government. It even conducts a printing operation in the basement of the Supreme Court Building in order to prepare guardedly, in advance, decisions of the Court and opinions of the justices.

4 GOVERNMENT PUBLICATIONS

A depository library system for government publications is based on a theory that information printed by the government should be distributed and kept permanently in every part of the country for citizens to consult. This notion is certainly fundamental to the American theory of democracy. In Jeffersonian terms, indeed, it is more easily justified than inexpensive mailing rates for pulp magazines.

A steep growth in the number of depository libraries has accompanied the proliferation of United States Government publications. The number of depository libraries is listed annually in the September issue of the *Monthly Catalog of United States Government Publications;* there are now approximately 1,100. As many as 300 of these have been added in the last decade and most represent the movement of junior colleges and community colleges to enlarge their library programs by acquiring government documents at no direct cost. This could be shortsighted for while the documents themselves are free, the expense of storage is high, and the easy acquisitions of these publications may not, in the long run, be beneficial in small institutions. In any event, the addition of depository libraries is in harmony with their steady growth since 1859 when a few depository libraries were begun under an act charging the Department of the Interior with the publication and distribution of government documents. National growth is evidenced by the dates on which libraries in the country were designated as depositories. The Boston Public Library, the Harvard University Library, and the Yale University Library all became depositories at the inception of the program. By 1900 depository libraries existed at the land-grant colleges, at most of the large city libraries in the country and at prominent private colleges. State libraries were also included in the program. The upshot is that these older libraries continue to have some edge on newer institutions.

Issued annually, the *United States Government Manual* contains several sections about the printing and publishing programs of the government. The description of the Government Printing Office mentions that a brochure, *How to Keep in Touch with U.S. Government Publications,* is available by writing to the Superintendent of Documents, Washington, D.C. 20402. In addition to six Government Bookstores in Washington, D.C., there are now stores in 15 other cities, listed in the *Manual.* Thus the *Monthly Catalog* and the *U.S. Government Manual,* (formerly the *U.S. Government Organization Manual),* taken with the classic guide *Government Publications and Their Use* by Schmeckebier and Eastin, will afford a sound beginning to working with the numerous sources that display the work of the departments and agencies in all three branches of the Federal government.

Since 1935 the *Government Manual* has been the "official handbook of the Federal Government" published by the Office of the Federal Register in the National Archives and Records Service of the General Services Administration. The *U.S. Government Manual* describes the purposes and programs of most government agencies, lists personnel, and provides brief statements of selected boards, commissions, and committees, the quasi-official agencies, and certain international organizations. In the span of a few pages it provides a basic picture of the organization being checked, a useful thing to have even though one knows that the political, legal, fiscal and social character of the organization is quite thoroughly left aside. The *Manual* describes and delineates even though all is done within the confines of bureaucratic blandness. Boxes in bold print now invite telephone calls for more information. The *Manual* is extremely useful for students and scholars tracing the myriad activities of government agencies, departments, bureaus and commissions. Great bedtime reading!

As an official Bible, the annual *U.S. Government Manual* is an exact, reliable handbook. It is not revealing about the Central Intelligence Agency and similar matters. The commercially done guide to *Government Publications* is a top-notch reference book.

6 GOVERNMENT PUBLICATIONS

The *U.S. Government Manual*, purporting to adhere to an annual July publishing date, has appeared months later on occasion. When the 1974-75 edition appeared in late November, 1974 it revealed a government in general as it appeared the previous July, but mirrored a sensible reality by listing members of the Executive Office of the President as of September, thus giving readers a Ford White House, rather than the Nixon one that had passed into the pale.

The *Monthly Catalog of United States Government Publications* is the basic bibliography to all government publications and an indispensable tool for anyone trying to keep in touch with or locate government publications. The first catalog was issued in January, 1895, and it has been published continuously since then under these titles:

a) *Catalogue of Publications Issued by the Government of United States* (January-March 1895)
b) *Catalogue of United States Public Documents, Issued Monthly* (April 1895-December 1905)
c) *Catalogue of United States Public Documents* (January 1906-June 1907)
d) *Monthly Catalogue United States Public Documents* (July 1907-December 1939)
e) *United States Government Publications Monthly Catalog* (January 1940-December 1950)
f) *Monthly Catalog of United States Government Publications* (January 1951-   )

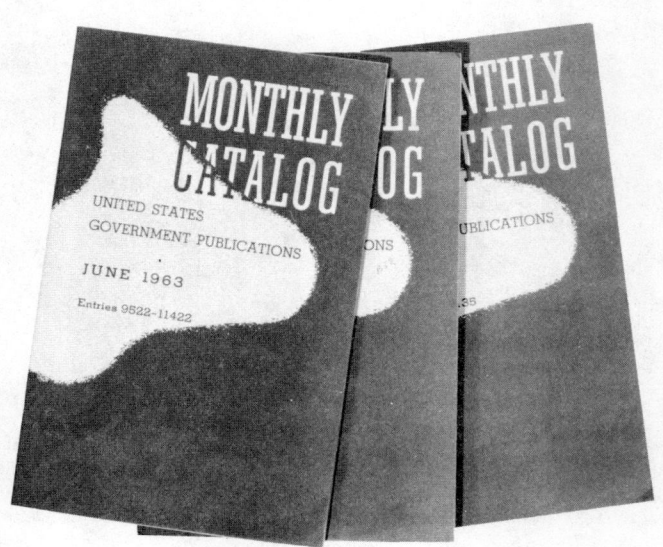

GOVERNMENT PUBLICATIONS 7

Each monthly issue now contains its own subject index, a personal author index, and a title index. There is also an annual cumulative index. A *Decennial Cumulative Index to the Monthly Catalog* for the years 1941 through 1950 was issued in 1953, and the *Decennial Cumulative Index, 1951-1960* appeared in 1969. Each February issue of the *Monthly Catalog* contains an Appendix entitled "Directory of United States Government Periodicals and Subscription Publications" which lists the title, an annotation, issuing agency, and subscription cost of Government periodicals. A convenient (and interesting) supplement to the *Monthly Catalog* is the monthly *Selected United States Government Publications* which lists publication and purchase information on new government titles of wide appeal or special importance. A lifetime subscription is available free from the Superintendent of Documents.

For government sources prior to 1940, students of political science would do well to consult these documents:

a) *A Descriptive Catalogue of the Government Publications of the United States, September 5, 1774-March 4, 1881*
b) *Comprehensive Index to the Publications of the United States Government, 1881-1893*
c) *Catalog of the Public Documents of the [53rd to 76th] Congress and of all Departments of the Government of the United States [for the Period of March 4, 1893 through December 31, 1940]*

The first of these, generally known as *Poore's Descriptive Catalogue, 1774-1881,* is the first and only attempt to make a complete list of all government publications: executive, legislative and judicial. The arrangement in the *Catalogue* is chronological; executive and judicial publications are found at the beginning of that portion relating to each year, followed by congressional documents consecutively listed by the date on which their printing was ordered. Each entry has an annotation, and there is a 148-page subject and name index.

The *Ames Comprehensive Index 1881-1893* (2 vols.) is a work arranged in three columns. The second column is the key work (subject) under which the documents are arranged alphabetically. The first gives the author or department issuing the document; the third is for documents in the Serial Set (see Congress chapter) and gives the Congress, session, document number and Serial Set volume number. There is a personal name index at the end of volume 2.

The *Ames* Index was superseded in 1893 by the *Catalog of the Public Documents of Congress and of All Departments of the Government of the*

8 GOVERNMENT PUBLICATIONS

United States [for the Period from March 4, 1893 through December 31, 1940] (known universally as the *Document Catalog*). This is an analytical dictionary with entries under subject and both individual and governmental authors. Issued biennially, each volume covers one Congress. The *Document Catalog* is the best and easiest source to use for locating government documents published from 1893 until 1940—after which the *Monthly Catalog* becomes the basic source. Included in the *Document Catalog* is a complete list of important Presidential orders and proclamations, departmental publications and periodicals, and Congressional publications. The *Document Catalog* was discontinued after 1940 to allow concentration on an expanded and more comprehensive *Monthly Catalog of the United States Government Publications.*

Bibliography

Ames, John Griffith. *Comprehensive Index to the Publications of the United States Government, 1881-1893.* 2 vols. Wash. D.C.: Govt. Prt. Off., 1905. Reproduced: Ann Arbor, Mich., Edwards, 1953. 2 vols. in 1.

Poore, Benjamin Perley. *A Descriptive Catalogue of the Government Publications of the United States, Sept. 5, 1774-March 4, 1881.* Compiled by order of Congress. Wash. D.C.: Govt. Prt. Off., 1885. Reproduced: Ann Arbor, Mich., Edwards, 1953.

Schmeckebier, Laurence F., and Eastin, Roy B. *Government Publications and Their Use.* 2d rev. ed. Wash. D.C.: The Brookings Institution, 1969.

U.S. Congress. *Congressional Record.* Wash. D.C.: Govt. Prt. Off., 1873-   . Contains proceedings and debates of the 43d Congress-March 4, 1873-   . Issued daily while Congress is in session.

U.S. Office of the Federal Register. *United States Government Manual.* Wash. D.C.: Govt. Prt. Off., 1934-. Official handbook of the Federal Government. Annual.

U.S. Superintendent of Documents. *Catalog of the Public Documents of the [53d to 76th] Congress and of all Departments of the Government of the United States [for the Period March 4, 1893-Dec. 31, 1940].* Wash. D.C.: Govt. Prt. Off., 1896-1945. Vols. 1-25.

_____. *Decennial Cumulative Index, 1941-1950.* Wash. D.C.: Govt. Prt. Off., 1953.

_____. *Decennial Cumulative Index, 1951-1960.* 2 vols. Wash. D.C.: Govt. Prt. Off., 1968.

_____. *Monthly Catalog of United States Government Publications.* Jan. 1895-   . Wash. D.C.: Govt. Prt. Off., 1895-   . Monthly.

_____. *Selected United States Government Publications.* 1972-   . Wash. D.C.: Govt. Prt. Off., 1972-   . Monthly.

2. The Constitution

One hardly needs to visit the shrine-vault containing the original handwritten Constitution in the National Archives Building in Washington to consult the greatest, most important single document for studying American government. It is faithfully reprinted in the *United States Government Manual,* most almanacs and many other places. Owing to the fact that the Constitution cannot safely be read without attention to the glosses put upon it by judges and others in the system and by the way in which the entire American system of government has evolved, guides to the text are needed by experienced lawyers and social scientists as well as students. Of all the guides there are, four call for mention here.

A classic reference book, *Edward S. Corwin's The Constitution and What It Means Today,* last prepared by our own Blackstone himself in 1958, was started up again in 1973. It is an annotated edition which is to say that the book is organized to provide an article-by-article, section-by-section, clause-by-clause commentary on meaning. The hard-cover edition is priced out of sight but the paper edition sells for less than $5.00 and, while there is an annual supplement, any copy will do very well for an undergraduate library. The fresh additions by Harold W. Chase and Craig R. Ducat can be recommended as in the spirit of the master. There are excellently written short essays, most notably the thirty pages entitled "The Warren Court and the Second Constitutional Revolution." There is a fine topical index indicating where one will find definitions and explanations of such terms as these: "absolutism as applied to civil liberties," "bill of attainder," "eminent domain," "inherent powers" and the "penumbra theory." Some 1500 cases are indexed in a separate table.

For scholars and students who want a "literal print" of the Constitution and then some, the best reference is *Constitution of the United States, Analysis and Interpretation,* commonly called the *Constitution Annotated.* The 1973 edition is available from the Government Printing Office for $20.50, a good buy. Prepared by the Congressional Research Service of the Library of Congress, this volume contains the full text of the Constitution, then reports it clause-by-clause with analyses of each one together with annotations of Supreme Court decisions. Also included in the volume are essays under the following titles: "Historical Note on Formation of the Constitution," "Proposed Amendments Not Ratified by the States," "Acts of Congress Held Unconstitutional in Whole or in Part by the Supreme Court of the United States," "State Constitutional and Statutory Provisions and Municipal Ordinances Held Unconstitutional on Their Face or as Administered," "Supreme Court

Decisions Overruled by Subsequent Decisions," and a "Table of Cases." It is much fuller than *Corwin's Constitution* by Chase and Ducat as shown by the fact that more than 6,000 cases are tabulated.

The enabling legislation (Public Law 91-589, 84 Stat. 1585, 2 U.S.C. sec. 168) took the form of a Joint Resolution authorizing this *Constitution Annotated* to describe pertinent decisions of the Supreme Court through to the end of its 1971-72 Term. Pocket supplements to the *Constitution Annotated* are to be added at the conclusion of the 1973-74, 1975-76, 1977-78, and 1979-80 Terms of the Supreme Court. The Joint Resolution then goes on to make this system permanent so that upon completion of the 1981-82 Term, "and upon the completion of each tenth October term of the Supreme Court thereafter, a hardbound decennial revised edition of the *Constitution Annotated"* shall be prepared and published. Up to this authorization there had been *ad hoc* support by Congress for editions beginning in 1920. Thus it is that an established library reference tool of inestimable value will now be available and may be subscribed to on a continuing basis.

Still other annotations of the Constitution are available in law libraries and in some large university libraries. One is in the *United States Code Annotated (U.S.C.A.)* by the West Publishing Company. The first nine volumes of the *U.S.C.A.* provide a distillation "of thousands of judicial interpretations of the Constitution in decided cases of both Federal and State Court." A topical index to the Constitution and descriptive word index to annotations and constructions in each section make for easy use. The Lawyers Cooperative Publishing Co.-Bancroft Whitney Co. publishes a similar annotation of the U.S. Constitution in two special volumes of its new *United States Code Service, Lawyers' Edition (U.S.C.S.).* One volume contains the pertinent historical documents and fundamental laws. A "literal text" of the Constitution is set out, followed by Articles I-III divided by section or clause. A subject analysis and annotations for each division are also provided.

A common drawback to these annotated Constitutions is their heavy stress on what the courts, especially the Supreme Court, have said about the meaning of the various clauses. The *United States Code Annotated* and the *United States Code Service* do this most, followed closely by the *Constitution Annotated.* The editors of *Corwin's Constitution and What It Means Today* pay somewhat more attention to such matters as impeachment proceedings which have not been subject to court rulings but where Congress has interpreted the Constitution without benefit of judicial review.

It is nevertheless true that all of these sources on the Constitution deal with each branch of the government so that there are ample treatments of the powers of Congress and of the President as well as of the Federal Courts. This means that as one considers the discussion of sources about these institutions in the pages that follow, the Constitution must be remembered as having a fundamental relationship to each.

Bibliography

Corwin, Edward S. *Edward S. Corwin's The Constitution and What it Means Today.* Revised by Harold W. Chase and Craig R. Ducat. 13th ed. rev. Princeton, N.J.: Princeton University Press, 1974.

United States Code Annotated. St. Paul, Minn.: West Pub. Co., 1967- . Cited as *U.S.C.A.* Cumulative, annual, pocket parts contain amendments and additions. Replacement volumes are issued from time to time.

United States Code Service, Lawyers' Edition. Rochester: Lawyers Co-operative Pub. Co.; San Francisco: Bancroft-Whitney Co., 1972- . Cited as *U.S.C.S.* Supplements, pocket parts and advance service pamphlets.

U.S. Library of Congress. *Constitution of the United States, Analysis and Interpretation.* Annotations of cases decided by the Supreme Court of the United States to June 29, 1972. Wash. D.C.: Govt. Prt. Off., 1973.

3. Congress

Congress is so record conscious that with 535 members, thousands of staffers, and millions of constituents, its work is necessarily characterized by an enormous variety of publications that are sped through the printing presses. In each two-year Congress there are more than 15,000 different bills with additional prints on many, all published quickly at the behest of the Representatives and Senators introducing them. There are also numerous committee prints, usually scholarly staff studies, as well as hearings, reports, calendars and guides to major legislative actions. These need to be examined by political scientists to learn about individual Congressmen, about the behavior of committees, about the process of legislation and so on. In fact there are numerous studies of Congress in print. Still, any student of the institution should be conversant with the basic reference series by and about Congress.

The publications of Congress are supplemented by commercial publications about Congress: its members, its processes, its results. The task faced by the student of Congress is to extract from these resources the pertinent data.

An appropriate point to begin a study of the reference tools on the Congress of the United States is with the sources on the men and women who make up this legislative assembly. One can easily find in any library numerous sources of information on particular United States Senators and Representatives, both past and present; but there are three sources which serve as a convenient starting place for anyone seeking biographical information on a Senator or a Representative, famous or infamous, important or obscure.

The first of these, the *Biographical Directory of the American Congress, 1774-1971*, updated every 10 years, contains more than 10,800 biographies of the elected or appointed members of the Continental Congress (1774-1788) and the Congress of the United States (1789-1971 inclusive). Arranged alphabetically, this *Biographical Directory* also includes biographies of the eight Presidents who never served as Members of Congress. Done in who's who style, there is little if any derogatory information. A macabre touch is the inclusion of the place of burial or interment for each deceased member. This also contains lists of the cabinet members (the Administration) of each President and the state delegations to each Congress which provides a means of reconstructing and of verifying historical associations.

Information on more current Members of Congress can be found in the "official" *Congressional Directory,* published annually, also by the G.P.O. A comprehensive and extensive book, it is a must for biographical and other pertinent information on the current Congress. The *Congressional Directory* includes biographies of Congressional members listed by state and an alphabetical listing of Senators and Representatives. It also includes information on the seniority and terms of service of the members, the Committees of the House and the Senate plus an alphabetical listing of Members' Committee assignments. Staff information for each Congress is provided as is a listing of the officers and personnel of the Senate, the House, and their Committees. Membership lists include those of Congressional Joint Committees, Commissions and Boards, Governors, and Foreign diplomatic Representatives. The principal administrative personnel of executive departments, independent agencies, international organizations, consular offices, and the District of Columbia also receive

The official *Congressional Directory,* published for decades, and the commercial *Staff Directory,* issued since 1959, appear early each year and compliment each other handsomely.

attention. Media representatives and services are listed; congressional district maps and miscellaneous statistical information are provided. The *Congressional Directory* is a handbook, in one volume, sometimes available from one's Congressman.

The final source of biographical information to students of Congress is the *Congressional Staff Directory,* published commercially. As its name would suggest, the *Staff Directory* contains over 1800 staff biographies on the "behind-the-scenes" faces to be found in the Capital. It also includes information on state delegations, on the staffs of the officers and committees of the Senate and the House of Representatives, and on executive department personnel.

While there are several unofficial sources and services which will give the student of public affairs an impressive coverage of the legislative process at work in Congress, the official documents used by Congress in its internal deliberations are readily available to students wishing or needing to track down details in so-called "primary sources." Most of these documentary items are a part of the material distributed to designated "depository libraries" by the Superintendent of Documents, and at least some are available in practically every college library in the country.

It would, however, be foolhardy to rush into a discussion of how to explore the legislative process in general and how to find legislative histories of particular bills without first understanding the basic documentary sources and publications of Congress. What follows is a brief introduction to these guides; the reader is urged to consult the revised and updated *How Our Laws are Made* for a fuller description. This is a pamphlet that may be obtained free from your Congressman.

Bills. A bill is the printed version of proposed legislation. It is introduced in either house of Congress by a member or members, and it is called a bill until it has been passed by the two houses and either approved by the President, not vetoed within the period fixed by the Constitution, or passed again over his veto. Today bills are numbered consecutively through an entire Congress, in separate series for each Congress and in each house, and the bill number provides a unique identification for the bill and for *all* hearings, reports, and action on it. Bills are initially printed as a "slip" bill; as the bill progresses through the legislative process, the bill is reprinted to reflect changes in its content.

Calendars. The *Calendars of the United States House of Representatives and History of Legislation* and the Senate's *Calendar of Business* are published daily when the Congress is in session. The *House Calendar* is the more comprehensive of the two and regularly provides a key to past and pending congressional business. More will be said about the *House Calendar* later, particularly about its function in seeking out legislative history.

Committee Hearings. The *Hearings* of the House and Senate contain the verbatim transcript of written or oral testimony given before House and Senate Committees and Subcommittees in public proceedings on proposed legislation, appropriations, investigations, etc. The Hearings are held by one or more committees of Congress on important bills to determine the desirability and kinds of legislation in particular (or general) areas. Hearings will frequently provide published and unpublished statements of organizations, agencies, and groups, statistical data and research, and reprints of germane articles. They can be extremely valuable sources of technical or "expert" information on the particular topic of the hearings. Those for one Congress will fill a large bay of shelves in a library.

Committee Reports. Each bill, when it is reported to the floor of the House or the Senate by the committee or subcommittee, is accompanied by a written "report" setting forth the recommendations of the committee together with explanations of the purpose and scope of the proposed bill and the reasons for its recommended approval. Committee recommendations are often accompanied by the supplemental, minority, or additional views of the committee members.

House and Senate Documents and the "Congressional Serial Set." Congressional Documents, in existence since 1817, are the studies and other miscellaneous material ordered printed by either house of Congress. Although the designation "Documents" often does not appear on the title page, when they are collected and issued (with the Committee Reports) Documents become part of the Congressional (or "Serial") Set. Among them are the investigative reports of congressional committees, monographs, Presidential messages, documents from executive departments and independent agencies, and material prepared for the use of the committee.

The two greatest functions of Congress, the deliberative and the law making, are recorded in two series of publications which date from the first Congress in 1789. Congress originally contracted with commercial printers for their publication and, while there has been some switching from time to time, there has never been a real break in the issuance of these two series of documents.

The laws passed by Congress are published chronologically in the *United States Statutes at Large* (about which more will be said later).

The debates and proceedings of Congress also have been published continuously but under different titles, and students of congressional activity would do well to consult these first when seeking the legislative history of a bill. The various forms the present *Congressional Record* has taken are: (a) *Annals of Congress;* (b) *Register of Debates;* (c) *Congressional Globe;* and (d) *Congressional Record.*

The first of these, the *Annals of Congress,* covers the debates and proceedings in the First Congress to the First Session of the Eighteenth Congress, 1789-1824. Unlike the present *Record,* the *Annals* were not contemporaneously reported; they are abstracts that were compiled in the nineteenth century. The last unit of the *Annals* for each Congress includes an appendix which contains the public laws and some executive reports. Each volume has separate indexes for House and Senate proceedings; however, neither is complete, so both should be consulted. These indexes are quite inadequate for some years, so the user should consult the appropriate volumes of the House and Senate *Journals* to supplement the shortcomings of the *Annals'* index. The *Journal* indexes will show on what dates action was taken, and these dates can then be consulted in the *Annals.*

From 1824 to 1837, i.e., from the Second Session of the Eighteenth Congress to the end of the First Session of the Twenty-fifth Congress, one can find in the *Register of Debates* a contemporaneously compiled abstract of the debates in Congress. The *Register* is not a verbatim report. Each volume of the *Register* has separate indexes for the Senate and House proceedings in each session, and the last unit for each session contains Presidential messages, departmental and committee reports, and the laws.

The *Congressional Globe* begins in 1833 with the First Session of the Twenty-third Congress (thus overlapping with the *Register of Debates)* and ends forty years later, 1873, with the Forty-second Congress. The *Globe,* after 1851, becomes more a verbatim account of the debates and less an abstract. It, too, has separate indexes for the Senate and House proceedings in each session. In addition, the appendix to each volume contains Presidential messages, reports of department heads, texts of laws, appropriation statements, and many speeches to which the debates make no reference.

The *Annals of Congress,* the *Register of Debates,* and the *Congressional Globe* were all published by commercial printers. In 1873 the Government Printing Office assumed the publication of the *Congressional Record* and it continues to do so today, a century later. The *Record,* frequently held up to ridicule for its wordiness, its inclusion of extraneous material published at the behest of Congressmen, and its genteel practice of permitting Members of Congress to change their remarks made on the floor after they have been spoken but before entry into the *Record,* is still

18 CONGRESS

The 30 books, above, are the 30 parts of a volume of the *Congressional Record* containing the debates in House and Senate for a single session of a recent Congress. Pagination is consecutive through the entire set. The final two parts contain, first, an index of remarkable detail and, second, a *Daily Digest* that is chronological. The chart at the right showing a "History of Bills Enacted" is one of the handy references to be found in the *Daily Digest* part of the *Congressional Record*.

CONGRESS 19

one of the publishing marvels of American government and politics. The *Record*, issued daily when Congress is in session, can be thought of as the world's largest daily newspaper on the grounds that it contains a daily verbatim account of everything said on the floor of both houses of Congress, extensive additional reprinting of national editorials and other comments, and a resume of congressional activity. After three bogus entries of remarks were published in the *Record* in 1974, the Speaker tightened verification rules to prevent such frauds and pranks. (See *Congressional Quarterly Weekly,* Aug. 31, 1974, pp. 2382-83.)

A summary of congressional activity with page references to the proceedings, the introduction, reporting, passage or approval of bills, was introduced in 1946 and is called the *Daily Digest* of the *Congressional Record.* The value of the *Digest* lies not only in its immediate use as a guide to hearings, bills reported, and so on; but also when the pages of the *Daily Digest* are brought together in a separate part of the permanently bound *Congressional Record* this part constitutes a veritable institutional diary. The bound *Daily Digest* includes a "Resume of Congressional Activity," a table of "Bills Enacted into Public Laws," and an elaborate and exceedingly valuable "History of Bills Enacted into Public Law," with

HISTORY OF BILLS ENACTED INTO PUBLIC LAW (87TH CONG., 2D SESS.)

Title	Bill No.	Date introduced	Committees—hearings		Date reported		Report No.		Page of Congressional Record of passage		Date of passage		Public law	
			House	Senate	House	Senate	House	Senate	House	Senate	House	Senate	Date approved	No.

details of activity at various stages of enactment and page references to final passage in the bound *Congressional Record*.

An additional aid to material in the *Record* is the fortnightly *Congressional Record Index* which includes a history of bills and resolutions for both the House and the Senate. This *Index* is also collated and bound as a separate part of the term. The *Index* volume of the *Record* contains an "Index to the Proceedings"—a general index by name and subject,—a "History of [Senate] Bills and Resolutions," and a "History of [House] Bills and Resolutions."

The *Congressional Record* provides the only extended account available of congressional deliberations. It also provides, in the *Daily Digest* and the *Index,* an invaluable aid for tracing the legislative history of a particular bill or law. For some research purposes a student of Congress may find it easier to use the *Senate Journal* and the *House Journal* in lieu of the *Congressional Record*.

Published pursuant to Article I, Section 5, Clause 3 of the United States Constitution which mandates that "[e]ach House shall keep a Journal of its Proceedings, and from time to time publish the same, excepting such Parts as may in their Judgment require Secrecy," the *Journals* record all actions taken, all motions, and the votes on roll calls and divisions. They do not include the debates. When researching a particular bill it is necessary to consult both the *Senate Journal* and the *House Journal* since neither *Journal* records action taken in the other house. The *Journals* are published at the end of a session, each house printing its entire proceedings in one volume, and thus they are of use only for past, not current, legislation.

For current legislation, an excellent source, in addition to the *Daily Digest* and the *Congressional Record Index,* is the *Digest of Public General Bills and Resolutions,* published since 1936 by the Congressional Research Service (formerly the Legislative Reference Service) of the Library of Congress. The *Digest* is published "during each session of a Congress in five or more cumulative issues with bi-weekly supplementation as may be needed and a final edition at the conclusion of each session."

Each cumulative issue describes its own contents in seven parts, as follows:

> Part I. *Status of Measures Receiving Action*—This part, in the second session of each Congress, also reflects action in the first session. Each measure which has become law is listed numerically by Public Law number. Other measures which have received action are listed thereafter by bill or resolution number. With respect to each

Public Law or other measure a digest is given as well as a brief legislative history indicating, as appropriate: (1) date reported; (2) report number; (3) dates considered; (4) dates passed; (5) conference action; and (6) approval date (or veto).

Part II. Public Law Listing—This contains a numerical listing of all enactments through the then current Congress indicating both the Bill and Public Law number.

Part III. Digests of Public General Bills and Resolutions—This includes digests (or, in some instances, a brief indication of the subject) of all Public Bills and Resolutions in numerical order as introduced; they are separately categorized, with respect to each House of Congress, as to Bills, Joint Resolutions, Concurrent Resolutions and Simple Resolutions.

Part IV. Sponsor Index—This index provides a reference, by subject, to all Public and Private Bills and Resolutions sponsored by each Member of Congress. A one-word or brief phrase description of the subject-matter of public measures is followed by the bill number or numbers pertaining to that subject entry. Private Bills are indicated under the entry "Private."

Part V. Subject-Matter Index—This index provides a reference to all public bills and resolutions in a given subject area. This index is preceded by a list of principal subject-matter headings under which detailed index entries thereafter may more readily be found. This list does not purport to be all inclusive. Measures which have received action and appear in either the Action or Public Law section are denoted by an asterisk.

Part VI. Specific-Title Index—This is an index of bills which contain a specific title. It is arranged alphabetically according to the first word of the title.

Part VII. Identical Bill Index—This includes all measures which are identical in both language and content. All such measures will appear under the number of the first such bill in the current session with cross references made for succeeding bills.

What the *Digest* lacks in current legislative history may well be found in the *Calendars of the United States House of Representatives and History of Legislation.* The *House Calendar* is issued daily when the House is in session, and it provides a cumulative history of bills in the Senate or in the House of Representatives. Included are sections on "Bills in Congress" (by date), "Bills Through Conference" (also by date), the various House Calendars, "Public Laws and Resolutions," and a section providing the "numerical Order of Bills and Resolutions which have passed either or both Houses, and Bills now pending on Calendars." A subject index is included once a week.

After the final adjournment of a Congress, a "Final Edition" of the *House Calendar* is issued. It contains all the information the daily *House Calendar* does with the addition of a comprehensive subject index. Although the "Final Edition" gives no information about the Bills and Resolutions on which the Senate or House took no action, it does provide an official list of bills which failed to become law either because of a Presidential veto while Congress was in session or a veto after the adjournment of Congress (a Pocket Veto).

The Senate's *Calendar of Business* is not nearly as extensive as the *House Calendar,* and one can find all the information the *Calendar of Business* contains in the *House Calendar.*

After checking with primary sources for the action taken on a particular bill, it is generally quite useful to examine the *Hearings. Hearings* do not comprise any regular series of Congress, and there is an absence of uniformity in their designation. They are published separately by the committee holding the hearings, and their titles usually reflect some aspect of the content of the material. Before a proper search can be made for the published record of hearings, note: (a) the name of the committee to which the bill was referred; (b) the number and session of the Congress during which hearings would have been held; and (c) the approximate date on which hearings would have been held.

The most comprehensive coverage early hearings can be found in these five volumes:

[1] *Index of Congressional Committee Hearings (not Confidential in Character) Prior to January 3, 1935, in the United States Senate Library.* (Wash. D.C.: Govt. Prt. Off., 1935)

[2] *Cumulative Index of Congressional Committee Hearings (Not Confidential in Character) From Seventy-Fourth Congress (January 3, 1935) through the Eighty-Fifth Congress (January 3, 1959) in the Senate Library.* (Indexed and compiled under the direction of F.M. Johnston by R.D. Hupman. Wash. D.C.: Govt. Prt. Off., 1959)

[3] *Quadrennial Supplement to Cumulative Index of Congressional Committee Hearings (Not Confidential in Character) from the Eighty-Sixth Congress (January 7, 1959) through the Eighty-Seventh Congress (January 3, 1963) together with Selected Committee Prints in the United States Senate Library.* (Compiled and indexed by Mary F.Sterrett. Wash. D.C.: Govt. Prt. Off., 1963)

[4] *Cumulative Index of Congressional Committee Hearings (Not Confidential in Character) Second Quadrennial Supplement from the Eighty-Eighth Congress (January 3, 1963) through the Eighty-Ninth Congress (January 3, 1967) together with Selected Committee Prints in the United Senate Library.* (Compiled under the direction of F.R.Valeo by Carmen Carpenter. Wash. D.C.: Govt. Prt. Off., 1967)

[5] *Cumulative Index of Congressional Committee Hearings (Not Confidential in Character) Third Quadrennial Supplement from the Ninetieth Congress (January 10, 1967) through the Ninety-First Congress (January 2, 1971) together with Selected Committee Prints in the United States Senate Library.* (Compiled under the direction of F. R. Valeo by Carmen Carpenter and Polly Sargent. Wash. D.C.: Govt. Prt. Off., 1971)

Two similar (but not identical) volumes with references to the holdings found in the Library of the United States House of Representatives are:

[1] *Index to Congressional Committee Hearings in the Library of the United States House of Representatives Prior to January 1, 1935.* (Compiled by Russell Saville. Wash. D.C.: Govt. Prt. Off., 1954)

[2] *Supplemental Index to Congressional Committee Hearings, January 3, 1949 to January 3, 1955: Eighty-First, Eighty-Second, and Eighty-Third Congresses, in the Library of the United States House of Representatives.* (Compiled by John A. Cooper. Wash. D.C.: Govt. Prt. Off., 1956)

Hearings, especially contemporary ones, may also be located in the *Monthly Catalog of U.S. Government Publications* where they are listed under the name of the committee as well as by subject. The earlier, biennial *Document Catalog* and the *Checklist of United States Public Documents, 1789-1909* also list hearings held prior to 1941. Finally, the *Checklist of Hearings before Congressional Committees through the 67th Congress* (compiled by Harold O. Thomen. Wash.: Government Printing Office, 1957-59) covers all hearings for which records have been found and indicates where the hearings can be located.

After hearings have been held, the pertinent committee or subcommittee sends its written report to the floor of the House or the Senate. Reports are numbered consecutively and will be cited by that number—the report number being completely different from the bill number. Since 1969 the number of the Congress has formed a part of the report number thus providing for easy and unique identification of any particular report.

Depository libraries receive the unbound reports as printed. Later the House and Senate Reports and the House and Senate Documents are reproduced in bound volumes and distributed as a separate series in a collection called the "Serial Set" or the "Congressional Set." This series is identified by its own serial number. To identify where in the Serial Set a particular report is located, it is necessary to look up the Congress and Report Number in the *Checklist of United States Public Documents, 1789-1909*, the *Document Index* (1895-1933), or the *Numerical Lists and Schedule of Volumes* (1933–   ) to find which of the more than 12,000 bound volumes of the Serial Set to retrieve.

Once a bill is passed by Congress and either signed by the President, passed over his veto, or simply held for 10 days (Sundays excepted) it becomes law as the Constitution provides. Public and Private Laws are numbered consecutively in chronological order of enactment. Since 1957, the number of the Congress forms the first part of the law number, thus providing easy identification to a Congress and its legislative output. Laws are published separately upon enactment in unbound form called "slip laws." Slip laws have, besides the law number, the Senate or House bill number, the official title of the law, its enacting clause, and the chapter number under which it will appear when superseded by publication in the *United States Statutes at Large,* the final, official chronological compilation of federal laws as they have been enacted. The final volume is issued annually and contains the laws enacted for each session of Congress.

The clarification of binding law and its publication for the information of all residents of the country have presented the most complex intellectual public policy and publishing task of Congress. The *Statutes at Large,* now past its 180th year of consecutive publication, contains too many additions, deletions and contradictions to make it a feasible key to the law in force for an accomplished lawyer, let alone an ordinary citizen. This is not to say that the *Statutes at Large* can be disregarded, only that its uses are limited. Congress recognized this difficulty and sought in 1873 to begin a codification of the laws in a series of publications called *Revised Statutes.* But there was insufficient appreciation of the difficulty of the task and also an unawareness of the stretch of time ahead that Congress should provide for in order to achieve a satisfactory codification. In a word, the *Revised Statutes* mudied rather than solved the problem for it became a series that stood beside the *Statutes at Large,* and weak editing produced numerous contradictions and difficulties for users. In the 1890s Congress appointed a commission which ultimately prepared the Criminal Code of 1909 and the Judicial Code of 1911 but, as Charles J. Zinn has pointed out, "Almost immediately after that Congress enacted laws which affected those codes but did not specifically amend them, again two bodies of law grew up side-by-side." (Zinn, "Codification of the Laws," *Law Library Journal* 45 [1952] 5.) Finally, in 1925 the first edition of the *United States Code* was adopted by Congress, and this as brought up-to-date now stands as a monumental yet relatively easy collection of books to use.

What had to be done by the codifiers was to work through the entire set of statutes in force at that time and to classify them under one of the fifty subject titles of the *Code*. The titles chosen were the most important subjects of legislation in 1925. While classification is a matter of opinion and judgment, the expert lawyers who have worked on the *Code* have done an impressive job. The *United States Code* has continued under a program of constant updating and revision with the result that today when a public law is enacted by Congress its place in a title of the *United States Code* is already settled.

The *United States Code* contains all the laws in force, organized by subject titles. It is an official publication and includes both a general index and an invaluable popular name index. The wayward may fear its provisions; students of American government should embrace the *Code*.

The *United States Code* is the official compilation of the law in force and it is printed and sold by the United States Government Printing Office. The *Code*, however, is, as we have seen, slow to be published and no interpretation is provided as to the meaning of these Congressionally enacted laws. The lack of judicial annotation to and construction of legislative statutes has led to the publication of two important annotated sources of law:

    United States Code Annotated (West Publishing Company)
    United States Code Service, Lawyers Edition (Lawyers Co-operative Publishing Co.–Bancroft Whitney Co.)

The first of these, *U.S.C.A.*, publishes in separate volumes each of the fifty titles of the official code. Each unit is kept current with an annual cumulative "pocket supplement." In addition, the *United States Code Annotated* includes, for each section, a digest of official and unofficial federal and state reports and the opinions of the United States Attorney General. There is an 8-volume index to the set as well as an individual index for each of the 50 titles.

The *Federal Code Annotated,* published by Bobbs-Merrill, was recently purchased by the Lawyers Co-operative Publishing Co-Bancroft Whitney Co. and has been rebound and retitled: *United States Code Service, Federal Code Annotated Edition.* The *U.S.C.S., F.C.A.* edition, in turn, is the starting point for the new *United States Code Service, Lawyers Edition.* Featured in the *U.S.C.S., Lawyers Edition* are:

— references to the rules and regulations of major governmental agencies found in the Code of Federal Regulations:
— analyses of pertinent court decisions citing all cases which "meaningfully construe or interpret the statute";
— references to other Lawyers Co-operative–Bancroft Whitney publications; and
— historical notes which trace the development of the law.

Up to this point our coverage of the Congress has centered chiefly on the official publications it generates. For the student who does not have access to all these documents, there are several publications which, because they are carefully documented, imaginatively edited, regularly published, thoroughly indexed, come with loose-leaf binders, are widely available in libraries and can be obtained by individuals at faculty and student rates, and are also heavily used by political scientists, merit extended comment.

A phenomenal range of political and legislative developments are covered in depth by the *Congressional Quarterly Weekly Report* published

by Congressional Quarterly, Inc. since 1944. This includes the full text of presidential press conferences and messages, details on lobbying expenditures, redistricting developments in every state, election campaigns, costs and results. The most important innovation of *Congressional Quarterly Weekly* was the careful preparation of roll call votes of all members of both Houses. These are not only published in the *Weekly Report* but compiled and separately published in the softbound *Congressional Roll Call*. In addition, they are compiled annually in a special single volume, *Congressional Quarterly Almanac*. In turn, the total studies produced by Congressional Quarterly have been published in volumes of longer range summaries called *Congress and the Nation:* the first covering the years 1945-1964; the second covering the Johnson Administration from 1965 to 1969; and the third covering Nixon's first term, 1969-1972. It is expected now this will be issued quadrennially.

Congressional Quarterly, Inc. also publishes the *Guide to the Congress of the United States,* a definitive one-volume work on the "origins and development" of the U.S. Congress, and *Current American Government,* an inexpensive, soft-bound, somewhat scattered handbook for students studying American government, and is intended for assigned reading in college courses. Congressional Quarterly really operates as a kind of research service, selling its words to regular newspapers throughout the country and placing its information in libraries as well. It is strong on objectivity, emphasizes up-to-dateness but regularly provides considerable depth in its reporting. Its very ample indexes have made it a service very highly regarded among political scientists.

A second notable service on Congress, designed particulary for lawyers, is the *United States Code Congressional and Administrative News,* a legal service pamphlet of the West Publishing Company of St. Paul, Minnesota. This is published every two weeks and includes the text of all public laws. In addition, selected official committee reports constitute the legislative history of these laws, and the *Congressional and Administrative News* also includes the text of presidential executive orders and proclamations and certain other key administrative rules and regulations. There is almost no editorial or descriptive comment in this publication, but it is a quick and useful text paralleling the *Statutes at Large* and the most important documents of Congress which pertain to the enactment of legislation. It too is collected and bound in annual volumes and consequently makes up an historical record since its initiation in 1940.

A different kind of service on Congress is the *Congressional Index* of Commerce Clearing House, Inc. This loose-leaf service is purely an index to legislation and treaties by subject, bill number, author, popular or "headline" legislation, and, after enactment, public law number. *Congressional Index* indicates the status of all House and Senate legislation including date of introduction, committee hearings and reports (if any), floor action and passage, and Presidential approval. The *Index* also provides information on voting and other miscellaneous data.

A new index and abstracting service begun in 1970 is the *Congressional Information Service: Index to Publications of the United States Congress.* CIS publishes a monthly *CIS Index* which "abstracts and indexes hearings, reports, committee prints, and other congressional papers issued during the previous month." There is a quarterly index cumulation with subject and name index; an index by bill, report, and document numbers; and an index to committee and subcommittee chairmen. The monthly publications are collated and published in an annual volume: *CIS/Annual.* This volume contains a legislative history, including all references found in the "Slip Law" to House Reports, Senate Reports, the *Congressional Record,* and all related hearings, House or Senate Documents, and Committee Prints, for all public laws enacted during the session.

One other source which deserves to be pointed out is called the *National Journal Reports* (previously *National Journal,* published by the Government Research Corporation), a weekly publication patterned on the CQ *Weekly Report* but emphasizing research and evaluative journalism resulting in substantial and detailed analysis of particular phenomena associated with Congress. Their in-depth stories may focus on lobbies, on a particular committee's work or on a particular public policy and deal with each in several pages. The *National Journal Reports,* begun in

1968, is now heavily depended upon by political scientists in the American government field who wish to have the kind of political science report on current events that ordinarily is available only after a scholar has worked on the subject. In common with the other commercial services dealing with Congress and with national government problems, the *National Journal Reports,* the *U.S. Code Congressional and Administrative News* and the Congressional Quarterly Service are each exceedingly expensive. While student subscriptions are available, the regular library fees for each run into the hundreds of dollars.

Bibliography

Commerce Clearing House, Inc. *Congressional Index.* 88th Cong.- . 1963- . Chicago.

Congressional Information Service. *CIS/Annual.* Part One: Abstracts of Congressional Publications and Legislative Histories. Part Two: Index of Congressional Publications and Public Laws. 1970- . Wash. D.C., 1971.

Congressional Quarterly Inc. *Congress and the Nation.* 1945-1972. Wash. D.C.: Vol. 1, 1945-1964; vol. 2, 1965-1968; vol. 3, 1969-1972. Issued quadrennially.

――――. *Congressional Quarterly Almanac.* 1945- . Wash. D.C. A compendium of legislation for one session of Congress. Published every spring.

――――. *Congressional Quarterly Weekly Report.* 1944- . Wash. D.C. Weekly.

――――. *Congressional Roll Call.* 1969- . Wash. D.C. A chronology and analysis of votes in the House and Senate. Annual.

――――. *Guide to Current American Government.* 1961/62- . Wash. D.C. Semiannual.

――――. *Guide to the Congress of the United States: Origins, History and Procedure.* Wash. D.C., 1971.

Congressional Staff Directory. Comp. and edited by Charles B. Brownson. Alexandria, Va., 1959- . Annual.

Government Research Corp. *National Journal Reports.* 1969- . Wash. D.C. Weekly.

United States Code Annotated. 1927- . St. Paul, Minn.: West Pub. Co. Cited as *U.S.C.A.* Cumulative, annual, pocket parts contain amendments and additions. Replacements volumes issued from time to time.

United States Code Congressional and Administrative News. 1941- . St. Paul, Minn.: West Pub. Co. Monthly. Cumulated for each session of Congress.

United States Code Service, Lawyers' Edition. 1972- . Rochester: Lawyers Co-operative Pub. Co.; San Francisco: Bancroft-Whitney Co.

U.S. Congress. *Annals of the Congress of the United States.* The debates and proceedings in the Congress of the United States. 1st Cong. through 18th Cong., 1st Sess., 1789-1824. Wash. D.C.: Gales and Seaton, 1834-1856.

———. *Biographical Directory of the American Congress, 1774-1971.* Wash. D.C.: Govt. Prt. Off., 1971. First issued in 1859.

———. *Congressional Globe.* Debates and proceedings of the Congress. 23d Cong. through 42d Cong., 1833-1873. Wash. D.C., 1834-1873.

———. *Congressional Record.* Proceedings and debates of the Congress. 43d Cong.- , March 4, 1873- . Wash. D.C.: Govt. Prt. Off. Issued daily while Congress is in session. *Index* volume issued at end of each session.

———. *Congressional Record Daily Digest.* 1947- . Wash. D.C.: Govt. Prt. Off. Annual issues are at the end of each session's *Congressional Record.*

———. *Official Congressional Directory for the Use of the United States Congress.* Wash. D.C.: Govt. Prt. Off., 1809- . Issued annually.

———. *Register of Debates in Congress.* 18th Cong., 2d Sess. through 25th Cong., 1st Sess., 1824-1837. Wash. D.C.: Gales and Seaton, 1825-1837.

———. *United States Statutes at Large.* 1789- . Vols. 1-12, 1789-1863. Boston: Little Brown & Co., 1861-1864. Vols. 13- . Wash. D.C.: Govt. Prt. Off., 1863- . Issued annually.

———. House. *Calendars of the United States House of Representatives and History of Legislation.* Published daily when Congress is in session. Cumulated at close of each Congress.

———. ———. *Journal of the House of Representatives of the United States.* 1789- . Wash. D.C.: Govt. Prt. Off.

U.S. House Committee on the Judiciary. *United States Code: 1970 Edition.* 15 vols. Wash. D.C.: Govt. Prt. Off., 1971. Containing the general and permanent laws of the United States, in force on Jan. 20, 1971. Arranged under 50 titles. Cumulative supplements issued annually. Supp. #3 covering 1973, 3 vols., issued 1974. Begun in 1924. Published every six years.

U.S. Congress. Senate. *Calendar of Business.* Issued daily while Congress is in session. Cumulated at close of each Congress.

———. ———. *Journal of the Senate of the United States of America.* 1789- . Wash. D.C.: Govt. Prt. Off.

U.S. Library of Congress. *Checklist of Hearings before Congressional Committees through the Sixty-Seventh Congress.* Comp. by Harold O. Thomen. Wash. D.C.: Govt. Prt. Off., 1957-1959.

_____. *Digest of Public General Bills and Resolutions.* 1936- . Wash. D.C. Annual cumulations.

U.S. Superintendent of Documents. *Checklist of United States Public Documents, 1789-1909.* 3d ed., rev. & enl. Wash. D.C.: Govt. Prt. Off., 1911. Reprinted by Kraus Reprint Corp., New York, 1962.

_____. *Index to the Reports and Documents. [Document Index]* 54th Cong., 1st Sess. through 72d Cong., 2d Sess., 1895-1933. Wash. D.C.: Govt. Prt. Off., 1897 to 1933. 43 vols.

_____. *Numerical Lists and Schedule of Volumes.* 1933- . Wash. D.C.: Govt Prt. Off. Annual.

Zinn, Charles J. *How Our Laws are Made.* Revised and updated by Joseph Fischer. Wash. D.C.; Govt. Prt. Off., 1971. 1st printing, 1953.

4. The Executive Branch

The Government of the United States is a giant among nations when judged by the quantity of its publications. The *Monthly Catalog of United States Government Publications,* the best guide to all government publications annually lists in excess of 30,000 entries. Of these, upwards of 90 per cent have their genesis in the Executive Branch.

A careful examination of the *Monthly Catalog* illustrates the extent and character of the documents available from the United States Government. Taken together, the *Monthly Catalog* and the *United States Government Manual,* the "official handbook of the Federal Government," provide researchers with a marvelous outline of Federal departments, offices, agencies, and, most importantly, with an appreciation of the breadth and depth of the books, pamphlets, reports and other publications available from the Federal bureaucracy. These two publications serve as a quick introduction at once to both the Federal Government and its publications.

Two other publications, however, are especially important to all citizens: the *Federal Register,* the daily news of Executive rules; and the *Code of Federal Regulations*, a subject cumulation of rules in force. Both are depository items available in designated libraries. These two series provide the text of Federal rules and procedures and other policies which govern the lives of all citizens and are a lawyer's best source of books for the general and permanent regulations of the Federal Government.

The *Federal Register* is "a uniform system for making available to the public regulations and legal notices issued by Federal agencies." The *Federal Register* describes in every issue its four major sections, as follows:

> I *Presidential Documents* which include Presidential Proclamations and Executive Orders
>
> II *Rules and Regulations* which contain "regulatory documents [of Executive agencies] having general applicability and legal effect most of which are keyed to and codified in the *Code of Federal Regulations"*

III *Proposed Rules* which contain "notices to the public of the proposed issuance of rules and regulations. The purpose of these notices is to give interested persons an opportunity to participate in the rule-making prior to the adoption of the final rules"

IV *Notices* which contain "documents other than rules or proposed rules that are applicable to the public. Notices of hearings and investigations, committee meetings, agency decisions and rulings, delegations of authority, filing of petitions and applications, and agency statements of organization and functions are examples of documents appearing in this section"

Authorized by an Act of Congress in 1935, the *Federal Register* began publication on March 14, 1936. It is published five days a week throughout the year. There are cumulative monthly, quarterly and annual indexes.

The *Code of Federal Regulations* is "the codification of the general and permanent rules published in the *Federal Register* by the Executive departments and agencies of the Federal Government." The *Code* is divided into 50 titles, some of them "reserved" for future use, each of which represents a broad area subject to Federal regulation. "Each Title is divided into Chapters which usually bear the name of the issuing agency. Each Chapter is further subdivided into Subchapters covering specific regulatory areas." There is an annually revised subject index to the *Code* contained in a separate volume entitled *General Index*. A *Finding Aids* volume will help the user locate statutory authority, rules, and Presidential Documents. The *Code of Federal Regulations* is kept up-to-date by the individual issues of the *Federal Register;* and these two publications, when used together, provide the latest version of any given rule.

The *Code of Federal Regulations,* ancillary volume entitled *Finding Aids* contains an eleven page "Guide to Federal Register Finding Aids." This table describes the various indexes and the numerical finding aids found in the publications of the Office of the Federal Register and indicates where they can be found. The "Guide" includes these five lists:

List A—Alphabetical List of Finding Aids
List B—Researching [Executive] Agency Materials
List C—Researching Presidential Materials
List D—Researching Statutory Materials
List E—Special Information Lists

The "Alphabetical List of Finding Aids" refers the researcher to a specific, numbered finding aid found in one of the publications which, in turn, provides a brief description of the aid and its location. The "Guide to

Federal Register Finding Aids" is a very useful source for those using any or all of the Federal Register System publications.

The President's power to issue executive orders, as it is to do all the things he does, stems from a number of sources, any number of which may come into play when he decrees some specific action. Most specific and most accountable for the bulk of executive orders recent Presidents have issued are the statutory obligations imposed by Congress. Price and Bitner in *Effective Legal Research* summarize the practice as follows: "Congress, within the very wide Constitutional limitations of the doctrine of separation of powers, may authorize the President to conclude reciprocal trade agreements with other nations; raise or lower tariff rates; withdraw public lands from private entry; fix certain prices; realign or create new federal agencies below the rank of department, and the like." "Presidential legislation," as Price and Bitner call it, consists of treaties and executive agreements, reorganization plans, proclamations, executive orders, and several categories of less important miscellaneous orders. But, they declare, "the most frequent and pervasive manifestation of the President's legislative activities is the issuance of proclamations and executive orders. They are the medium through which the President exercises a great deal of his authority, especially that delegated to him by Congress through specific legislation. In importance they vary from the order authorizing the appointment of a minor government employee without regard to Civil Service rules, to those establishing war emergency agencies such as the Office of Price Administration and fixing its functions. Revocation, superseding, or amendment of an order is by another such order." (Price & Bitner, *Effective Legal Research,* p. 144.)

Although specifically delegated tasks by Congress account for most of the approximately 100 executive orders issued each year in recent times, the more noteworthy Presidential orders tend to be more broadly based. They rest in part on some stated Congressional authorization, but go on to assert power stemming from the Constitution itself, such as President Ford's blanket pardon of Richard M. Nixon on September 9, 1974, perhaps in keeping with Presidential obligations as Commander-in-Chief, and as one who is charged with the constitutional duty to "take care that the laws be faithfully executed . . ."

Until 1936 all proclamations, such as Lincoln's Emancipation Proclamation in 1862 and 1863, and executive orders were published in the *United States Statutes-at-Large.* All were issued, also, in slip form by the State Department.

Not until 1907 were orders and proclamations numbered, but in that year an unsung but numerically inclined clerk in the State Department assigned numbers to all those previously issued, and then instituted a practice of continuing the numbers, in separate series for proclamations and executive orders, consecutively for all Presidents. The appearance of the *Federal Register* as a daily publication for the executive branch of the government on March 14, 1936, provided a regular outlet for proclamations and executive orders. The first to appear was Executive Order Number 7316 issued by President Franklin D. Roosevelt. President Truman's first order was numbered 9538. The *Federal Register* is the first place, the most official place, but it is not the most convenient place to locate Presidential Executive Orders and Proclamations. That place is the annual supplements and four year compilations of Title 3 of the *Code of Federal Regulations.* This amplifies Title 3—The President—in the *United States Code,* and is readily and cheaply available from the Government Printing Office and, of course, in many libraries.

In assaying a President's work it is important to locate the precise order and language used to accomplish his purpose. Those more than a year old will be found in both Title 3 cumulations of the *Code of Federal Regulations,* as well as in the daily *Federal Register.* Thus on February 19, 1942 by Executive Order 9066 did Franklin D. Roosevelt set up the legal basis for interning Japanese-American citizens during World War II. The Order is entitled "Authorizing the Secretary of War to Prescribe Military

The *Code of Federal Regulations,* Title 3, includes all Executive Orders of the Presidents since 1936 while the *Public Papers* series includes press conferences.

Orders," and the parallel citations are 7 Fed. Reg. 1407 and 3 C.F.R 1938-1943 Compilation 1092.

The *Public Papers of the Presidents of the United States* is a series of volumes begun in 1957 in response to a recommendation of the National Historical Records Commission. There had been no uniform publication of Presidential papers until that time. While James D. Richardson had assembled messages and papers covering the period from 1789 to 1897 at the end of the last century and private compilations, such as those for Franklin D. Roosevelt edited by Samuel Rosenman, had been issued, there was no systematic publication comparable to the *Congressional Record* or the *United States Reports* for the Supreme Court.

This handsome series, with distinctive spines for the volumes of each President, is keeping up with the present, with the final Richard Nixon volumes scheduled for publication early in 1975. This will complete a series of annual volumes for the years 1945 to 1974 containing the papers of Presidents Truman, Eisenhower, Kennedy, Johnson and Nixon.

In 1972, government publication of the papers of President Herbert Hoover from March 4, 1929 to March 4, 1933 and those of President Franklin D. Roosevelt from 1933 to 1945 were authorized. It will take some time before all of these volumes appear. The 1929 Hoover volume was published on his centenary in 1974 and its organization displays fully the worthiness of this ambitious project. President Hoover's news conferences are published in this volume for the first time in full text because, at the time they were held, direct quotation of the President's replies were often not authorized. The list of items is presented chronologically. Item No. 1 is Hoover's inaugural address and this volume will henceforth be the best, official citation for it as well as for Item No. 257 titled "Statement on the National Business and Economic Situation," dated October 25, 1929, which begins with a famous reassurance: "The fundamental business of the country, that is the production and distribution of commodities, is on a sound and prosperous basis." There is at the conclusion of Hoover's remarks a short editorial note: "On October 24, Black Thursday, nearly 13 million shares had been traded on the New York Stock Exchange. October 29 would become Black Tuesday, the date commonly taken as the beginning of the Great Depression." (p. 356) The *Public Papers of the Presidents* generally are executed with high editorial standards and are now standard to all adequate library collections on American government.

Because Executive Orders had had no regular place of publication prior to the establishment of the *Federal Register* and the *Code of Federal Regulations* in the mid-thirties, a companion volume containing those of President Hoover was issued in 1974 with his 1929 *Papers*. It is entitled *Proclamations and Executive Orders, Herbert Hoover, 1929-1933*.

For current, accurate and full texts about actions at the White House, the *Weekly Compilation of Presidential Documents* is a gem. It makes available transcripts of the President's news conferences, messages to Congress, public speeches and statements, and other Presidential material released by the White House up to 5 p.m. of each Friday. Also prepared by the Office of the Federal Register, the *Weekly Compilation* is published each Monday.

The *Weekly Compilation of Presidential Documents* has gradually evolved since it was begun in 1965 to be equivalent to the *Congressional Record* in its latitude and informality. The transition issue dated Monday, August 12, 1974, for example, starts early the previous week with statements by Ron Ziegler and Vice President Ford that are bland and misleading, following with the revealing statements of Senators Goldwater and Scott and Representative Rhodes meeting with the press, the resignation speech and maudlin talk to the White House staff by President Nixon, the brief, official letter of resignation of Nixon and the swearing in of Ford, and concluding with the first utterances of Gerald R. Ford as the thirty-eighth President of the United States. While this is an extraordinary issue, the *Weekly Compilation* is consistently thorough and well-indexed and outdistances every other source, including its closest rival, the *Congressional Quarterly Weekly,* in documenting the President's official life.

There is a distinction between the *Weekly Compilation* and the *Public Papers* that is crucial to bear in mind. It is that the former includes whatever the White House press officer releases that week, and it is a generous amount of extraneous material. During the last months of Nixon's term in office, for instance, the *Weekly Compilation* included the text of several statements and briefs prepared by his lawyer, James D. St. Clair. Librarians will wish to preserve all of the numbers of the *Weekly Compilation* through the years as a basic source which contains remarkable immediacy, poignancy and completeness about the Presidential environment. The *Public Papers of the Presidents,* on the other hand, is limited to the utterances of the man in the White House. It is prescribed that the "basic text of each volume shall consist of oral statements by the President or of writings subscribed by him." (37 Fed. Reg. 23607, Nov. 4, 1972.)

A guide to the vast literature on the Presidency is the uncritical but convenient *The Presidents of the United States 1789-1962.* This bibliographical publication of the Library of Congress includes works of collective biography and books on the Presidency, Presidential elections, the White House, and the Vice Presidency. Each President's published writings and papers are listed along with the leading biographical books and articles.

The *Constitution Annotated* (See United States Constitution) contains more than 100 pages on the national executive and treats tenure, succession, the commander-in-chief, pardons, executive agreements, removal power, the legislative role of the President, and impeachment.

Other publications by the Executive Branch include the *Budget of the United States* and the *Economic Report of the President.* In addition, Presidential advisory boards, committees, councils and commissions, ordinarily established by Executive Order to scrutinize a particular problem and to make recommendations for action to the President, often generate reports which are readily available to the public.

Detailed explanations and reviews of Administration policy in specific areas are often set forth in the publications of the Executive Departments. Annual Reports by the Attorney General for the Department of Justice, by the Department of State and the Department of Defense review in detail the prominent events of the year. Similar reports are available for most Executive departments, agencies and offices.

The Federal bureaucracy is so large that a student unfamiliar with its complexities and character will learn much by examining the *U.S. Government Manual* and then using the card catalog of a good library. This will lead to reports, periodicals, and specialized publications of the department, agency or unit being studied. Secondary sources will also turn up books about the particular institution. If periodical sources are also consulted, biographical information about present and former administrators will afford further data. Thus, an inquiry into the Federal Bureau of Investigation would turn up items in the card catalog such as the *FBI Crime Reports,* the *Annual Report of the Attorney General* and books like *Kennedy Justice* by Victor Navasky. A related approach should be made by searching for books on J. Edgar Hoover, and this should be pursued in the periodical and biographical indexes as well as in the card catalog.

Because most publications of the Government Printing Office are listed in the *Monthly Catalog of U.S. Government Publications* under "government authors," usually the issuing agency, it is difficult to locate individual reports to the President or other reports that have been identified publicly and popularly with an individual name. It was only in January 1963 that the *Monthly Catalog* began to index personal author entries. An example of a "government author" is the Office of the Federal Register in the instance of the *Public Papers of the Presidents.* More often than not the name of a prominent individual associated with a report might not be mentioned in the title, text or biographical reference to it. A slender and inexpensive G.P.O. publication prepared in the Library of

Congress called *Popular Names of U.S. Government Reports: A Catalog*, first issued in 1966 and updated in 1970 fills this void. By turning to this, one can find the "Adams Report" on weights and measures dated 1821, the 1931 "Wickersham Report" on Prohibition, and the "Warren Report" on the assassination of President Kennedy.

Bibliography

Navasky, Victor S. *Kennedy Justice.* New York: Atheneum, 1971.

Public Papers and Addresses of Franklin D. Roosevelt, The, 1928-1945. With a special introduction and explanatory notes by President Roosevelt. Comp. by Samuel I. Rosenman. New York: Random House, 1938-[50]. 13 vols.: vols. 6-9 Macmillan; vols. 10-13 Harper.

U.S. Federal Bureau of Investigation. *Uniform Crime Reports for the United States,* 1930- . Annual.

U.S. Justice Department. *Annual Report of the Attorney General.* 1870- Wash. D.C.: Govt. Prt. Off., 1870- . Annual.

U.S. Library of Congress. *The Presidents of the United States 1789-1962: A Selected List of References.* Comp. by Donald H. Mugridge. Wash. D.C.: Govt Prt. Off., 1963.

_____ . *Popular Names of U.S. Government Reports. A Catalog.* 1966- Rev. & enl., 1970. Wash. D.C.: Govt Prt. Off.

U.S. Office of Management and Budget. *The Budget of the United States Government* and *The Budget of the United States Government—Appendix.* Wash. D.C.: Govt. Prt. Off., 1962- . Annual. Previously published as a Senate document.

U.S. Office of the Federal Register. *Code of Federal Regulations.* Dec. 31, 1948- . Wash. D.C.: Govt. Prt. Off., 1949-

_____ . *Federal Register.* March 14, 1936- . Authorized by act of July 26, 1935. Wash. D.C.: Govt. Prt. Off., 1936- . Daily except Sat., Sun. and official Federal holidays.

_____ *Public Papers of the Presidents of the United States.* Containing the public messages, speeches and statements of the President. Wash. D.C.: 1957- . Annual.

_____ . *Weekly Compilation of Presidential Documents.* Vol. 1, no. 1, Aug. 2, 1965- . Wash. D.C.: Govt. Prt. Off., 1965- . Weekly.

U.S. President. *Economic Report of the President.* Transmitted to Congress together with annual report of Council of Economic Advisors. 1947- Wash. D.C.: Govt. Prt. Off., 1947- . Annual.

———. *A Compilation of the Messages and Papers of the Presidents, 1789-1897.* Comp. by James D. Richardson by authority of Congress. 10 vols. Wash. D.C.: Govt. Prt. Off., 1896-1899.

U.S. Superintendent of Documents. *Monthly Catalog of United States Government Publications.* Jan. 1895-   . Wash. D.C.: Govt. Prt. Off., 1895-   . Monthly.

5. Federal Courts

The *United States Reports* from 1790 to the present, and continuing, are indispensable for students of constitutional law and of judicial behavior. Thus the compiler of a constitutional law textbook would ordinarily use little else besides the opinions found in the *United States Reports*. The *United States Reports* are not only essential in charting the development of constitutional doctrine, the judicial philosophies of individual justices or of whole courts as they appear in the opinions, but they also have been crucial in some of the pathbreaking intellectual work in political science on judicial behavior. For example, the work of C.H. Pritchett, represented particularly in his *Roosevelt Court* (Macmillan, 1947), was accomplished by his almost exclusive use of the *United States Reports* as his study laid bare the division among the justices registered in these volumes. Thus the official decisions of the Court are not only useful in historical and conventional descriptions of the Court but also in ascertaining the social and political dynamics among the justices.

One further point should be made about the overarching significance of the *United States Reports* as a source in understanding the work of the Supreme Court. This series includes the orders of the Court and all of the petitions that are received by it. This feature, a summary of the Court's proceedings and announcements, called the *Journal of the Supreme Court*, is incorporated in the *Reports*. Consequently it is a starting point for numerous types of intellectual enterprise. Many observations predicting the future course of decision begin with attention to details in the opinions. Detective work in the *U.S. Reports* often tells a great deal about the Supreme Court as an institution. The bound volumes are preceded by regularly issued "advance sheets" each Term.

The opinions of the Supreme Court in decided cases are prepared individually and published on the day of the decision in the form of a separate pamphlet or sheet for each opinion or order. These "slip" opinions are later republished in booklets called "Preliminary Prints" or "Advance Sheets" of the *United States Reports* and contain not only the opinions, but names, counsel, and editorial additions. Finally, the official bound volumes of the Preliminary Prints are published each term by the Government Printing Office in about four numbered volumes.

Most college libraries possess the *United States Reports* as they are "depository" items of the United States Government Printing Office. The power, prestige, and magic of the Supreme Court of the United States are reflected in the fact that four commercial publishers reprint the *United States Reports* verbatim as the basis of publications known as law reporters they offer for sale, and successfully so, to lawyers and others, political scientists among them, who follow legal developments. Larger libraries will have these and it is well to be aware of them. They are: *The United States Law Week, United States Supreme Court Reports, Lawyers Edition, Supreme Court Reporter,* and the *United States Supreme Court Bulletin.*

From its beginning in 1789 the rulings and opinions of the Supreme Court have been published in a series entitled *United States Reports,* one of the more than 400 volumes so far being shown on the left. The importance of the Court is shown by the fact that commercial publishers succeed in selling parallel sets, each with some attractive editorial embellishments. The *Lawyers' Edition* summarizes each case as well as briefs of counsel and contains annotations, or essays, on the state of the law when significant decisions are announced. The *Supreme Court Reporter* is keyed to general rules of law in digests that are much used by lawyers. The *U.S. Law Week* reports on the docket and oral arguments (as shown to the right at page 45) and the CCH *Bulletin* also keeps up-to-date on the history of cases on the docket. Small libraries need only the *United States Reports;* only law libraries would have all five of these parallel reporters.

Political scientists find these "unofficial" reports of the Supreme Court substantially more useful than the official *Reports* because of the inclusion of abstracts of briefs in some, the excerpts from oral arguments in others, the headnotes and summaries of opinions in all, and annotations and review articles. Thus the addition of these "unofficial" reports to the *United States Reports* is a sensible investment for a college library. As duplicate sets are built, too, casebooks can be laid aside and all students can read the important decisions in the original.

The United States Law Week is the single most complete source on current developments in the Supreme Court. Published since 1933 by the Bureau of National Affairs, Inc., *U.S. Law Week* is a two-volume weekly service consisting of sections on the Supreme Court and General Law. The opinions of all Supreme Court cases are photographed and mailed to subscribers every decision day. Summaries of all docketed cases are printed. The status of each case on the docket can thus be easily ascertained. The *Journal of the Supreme Court* is reprinted with its schedule of actions or motions and oral arguments. In addition, there are special articles on the Court's work, including summaries of arguments in important cases and periodical reports on cases argued and awaiting decision. The "General Law Section" gives synopses of significant decisions by all federal or state courts and be federal agencies.

These two pages of *United States Law Week* suggest the detail to be found in this expensive looseleaf service that anyone can use with patience and attentiveness. As the Supreme Court is now asked to review more than 5,000 cases a term, this service is perfect if one wishes to keep track of specific cases.

The *Lawyers Edition of the United States Supreme Court Reports* contains every case decided by the Supreme Court since 1790. The cases are reported in full, and the majority, dissenting, and separate opinions are summarized and headnoted. Headnotes are classified to the *United States Supreme Court Digest Annotated.* (The *United States Supreme Court Digest Annotated* is an "18 volume set containing a digest, a word index to the digest, a table of cases, tables of statutes cited and construed, two volumes of rules of court and, in an unnumbered volume, an Index to Annotations." Also provided by LCP-BWC.) Summaries of the briefs of counsel are also provided. "Advance Sheets" of the *Lawyers Edition* are published bi-weekly while the Court is in session and provide a rapid means of getting Court decisions as soon as they are available. They carry headnotes, summaries of the opinion in each case, and other explanatory aids.

The *Supreme Court Reporter,* a part of the "National Reporter System" of the West Publishing Company, is another source of the United States Supreme Court decisions. It begins with the October, 1882, Term. Each case in the *Supreme Court Reporter* is broken down into the West "Key Number System," one of the most audacious, and successful, indexing systems in existence. The National Reporter System embraces all of these publications in addition to the *Supreme Court Reporter:*

Federal Reporter (300 volumes)—the chronological series of decisions in lower Federal Court cases from 1880-1924;

Federal Reporter, 2nd Series—currently the official publication of the U.S. Court of Appeals, the U.S. Court of Claims, and the U.S. Court of Customs and Patent Appeals; and

Federal Supplement—since 1932 a series of reports for selected U.S. District Court and U.S. Custom Court decisions.

A complete set of state and federal decisions is really inappropriate for a college library. However, some may find a useful substitute in the still quite massive *American Law Reports.* This publication of the Lawyers' Co-operative Publishing Co.-Bancroft-Whitney Co. provides the texts of important opinions of appelate courts in all jurisdictions. (A minimum of United States Supreme Court cases is included as these are covered by the annotation in the *Lawyers Edition of the United States Supreme Court Reports.*) The *American Law Reports,* known as *A.L.R.,* is an up-to-date compilation of annotations—"each a complete and detailed treatise on a practical point of current law, each preceded by a report in full of a modern case from a state or federal appelate court involving the problem annotated"—which can cut the number of reports a small library needs.

For the student or scholar with a specific legal problem to be researched, reference should be made to the so-called "loose-leaf" services. These services, whose publishers include the Bureau of National Affairs, Inc., Commerce Clearing House, and Prentice-Hall, each relate to a specific topic and provide up-to-date decisions and regulations on that topic. All pertinent new material—court decisions, independent administrative agency rulings, etc.—is synthesized to insure that the user is familiar with all the new developments in the field.

When the legal terminology being used becomes a problem, reference to a dictionary is advised. Courts today officially rely on *Webster's Third New International Dictionary* (1969). This unabridged dictionary defines obscure as well as the most frequently used words in legal writing. (See chapter on Political Dictionaries.)

The mark of a "law dictionary" is its citation of words used in the context of actual judicial opinions. James Bouvier of Pennsylvania in the 1830s created the first law dictionary to quote largely from American opinions. *Black's Law Dictionary* or *Ballentine's Law Dictionary, with Pronunciations* are in this tradition.

Other, miscellaneous sources on the Court include The Oliver Wendell Holmes Devise *History of the Supreme Court of the United States* scheduled to be in twelve volumes. Edited by Harvard Law School

Professor Paul A. Freund, these volumes are the result of legislation (P.L. 84-246) which specified that the principal purpose of Holmes' $263,000 bequest would be the preparation and publication of a history of the Supreme Court of the United States. As of 1974 only three volumes had appeared, but the series thus far is sufficiently impressive to recommend the acquisition of the set by most college libraries.

For locating articles and books on specific subjects, reference should be made to the H. W. Wilson Company's *Index to Legal Periodicals.* Also of interest is the Jones and Chipman work for the years 1803-1937, *Index to Legal Periodical Literature.* The Harvard Law Library's *Annual Legal Bibliography* originated in 1961, and includes books and articles received by that library on domestic and foreign law. In addition, the *Harvard Law Review* surveys the past term of the Supreme Court in detail each year—usually in the November issue. Finally, *The Supreme Court Review*

The Supreme Court is governed, first, by the Constitution's Article 2, then, by Congressional Judiciary Acts in the *United States Code*'s Title 28 and, thirdly, by its own rules. The *Revised Rules of the Supreme Court,* in the pamphlet above, can be obtained from the Clerk. The books on *Briefing and Arguing Federal Appeals* and *Supreme Court Practice* are informative manuals on the handling of litigation.

of the University of Chicago Law School faculty (edited by Philip B. Kurland), published annually since 1961, is a one-volume collection of articles addressed chiefly to the latest Term. This is, of course, but one of about 200 law reviews, and its articles, like those in the reviews prepared by law school students, may be exploited by using the *Index to Legal Periodicals* and the Interlibrary Loan System.

In-depth legal research should begin with and will be aided by one of the superior books on the study of law. Price and Bitner's *Effective Legal Research,* Pollack's *Fundamentals of Legal Research,* Roalfe's *How to Find the Law,* and Cohen's *Legal Research in a Nutshell* are all excellent sources which describe the sources of statute and administrative decisions as well as judicial rulings. Students should use them to learn the many specific points about the law library that are beyond the scope of this publication.

Bibliography

American Law Reports. 3d. 1965- . Rochester: Lawyers Co-operative Pub. Co.; San Francisco: Bancroft-Whitney Co.

Annual Legal Bibliography. Vol. 1, 1960/1961- . Harvard Law School Library. Cambridge, Mass. Annual.

Ballentine, James Arthur. *Ballentine's Law Dictionary, with Pronunciations.* 3d ed. Edited by William S. Anderson. Rochester: Lawyers Co-operative Pub. Co., 1969.

Black, Henry Campbell. *Black's Law Dictionary.* 4th rev. ed. St. Paul, Minn.: West Pub. Co., 1970.

Cohen, Morris L. *Legal Research in a Nutshell.* St. Paul, Minn.: West Pub. Co., 1968.

Federal Reporter. March 1880-Nov. 1924. 300 vols. St. Paul, Minn.: West Pub. Co., 1880-1925.

Federal Reporter, 2d Series. Vol. 1, Nov. 1924- . St. Paul, Minn.: West Pub. Co.

Federal Supplement. Vol. 1, Oct. 1932/Feb. 1933- . St. Paul, Minn.: West Pub. Co.

Harvard Law Review. Vol. 1, 1887- . Cambridge, Mass. Monthly except July-Oct.

History of the Supreme Court of the United States. The Oliver Wendell Holmes Devise. General editor, Paul A. Freund. New York: Macmillan Co. 12 vols. in set. Vols. 1, 5 and 6 issued as of 1974.

Index to Legal Periodical Literature. Vols. 1-6. Vols. 1-2 edited by Leonard A. Jones; Vols. 3-6 by Frank E. Chipman. Boston: Boston Book Co., 1888-1919. Chipman, 1924. Indianapolis: Bobbs-Merrill, 1933. Los Angeles: Parker and Baird, 1939.

Index to Legal Periodicals. 1908- . Published for the American Association of Law Libraries. New York: H. W. Wilson Co., 1909- .

Kurland, Philip B., ed. *The Supreme Court Review.* 1961- . The Law School, The University of Chicago. Chicago and London: Univ. of Chicago Press. Annual.

Pollack, Ervin Harold. *Fundamentals of Legal Research.* 3d ed. Brooklyn, N.Y.: Foundation Press, 1967.

Price, Miles O.; and Bitner, Harry. *Effective Legal Research.* 3d ed. South Hackensack, N.J.: Rothman Reprints, 1969. Reprint of 1953 ed.

Roalfe, William R., ed. *How to Find the Law.* 6th ed. St. Paul, Minn.: West Pub. Co., 1965.

Supreme Court Reporter. Oct. 1882 term- . St. Paul, Minn.: West Pub. Co.

United States Law Week, The. A National Survey of Current Law. Vol. 1, Sept. 5, 1933- . Wash. D.C.: Bureau of National Affairs, Inc. Weekly.

U.S. Supreme Court. *United States Reports.* Cases adjudged in the Supreme Court. Vol. 1, Sept. 1754- . Wash. D.C.: Govt. Prt. Off.

United States Supreme Court Bulletin. 1957- . Chicago: Commerce Clearing House.

United States Supreme Court Digest Annotated. 1948- . 18 vols. Rochester: The Lawyers Co-operative Pub. Co; San Francisco: Bancroft-Whitney Co. Annual pocket supplements.

United States Supreme Court Reports, Lawyers Edition. Rochester: The Lawyers Co-operative Pub. Co.; San Francisco: Bancroft-Whitney Co. Vol. 1, 1790-Oct. term 1955. 2nd series, vol. 1, Oct. term 1956- .

Part Two:

General Reference Books

6. Almanacs

"Never underestimate the intelligence of an undergraduate," a distinguished political science professor once said, "but never *overestimate* his grasp of the facts." *The World Almanac and Book of Facts,* so named because it was first published by the *New York World* in 1868, is an enormous publishing success, as shown by its many imitators. Its journalistic roots (it is now published by the Newspaper Enterprise Association) register even today in its bulk of 1040 pages, cheap newsprint, sales at newsstands, drug stores and supermarkets as well as bookstores, and its somewhat bewildering practice of predating each edition. Thus does *The World Almanac and Book of Facts for 1974* include a section titled "Late News, Addenda, Changes" which includes items dated between August 2 and October 28. The items are keyed into topical sections in the book, particularly to chronology of the year's events from November 1, 1972 to November 1, 1973. The retrospective information with the prospective date is not deceit: it is simply a trait common to most pulp-paper almanacs and with the key sales period that coincides with the Christmas spirit.

The World Almanac and its rivals bring together most of their facts from government publications with the source identified. Information about the nations of the world and the states of the union are old standbys as are biographical sketches of American Presidents and their wives. The statistical information drawn from the official censuses of population, business, agriculture and so on is voluminous. There is heavy coverage of recent elections in the U.S.A. but not elsewhere, and there is no attention paid at all to public opinion polls or survey research data. Chronologies are great favorites, with memorable dates from 3000 B.C. to last year in one section and a day-by-day listing for the most recent 12 month period. Although disasters, dams, railroads, air flights, shot put and javelin records are here by the score, it is worth noting that, like newspapers, there are typographical errors, and the publishers protect themselves against suit by stating firmly at the outset that "The World Almanac does not decide wagers" (106th ed., 1973, p. 35).

The two almanacs that otherwise sell best and have the closest affinity to *The World Almanac* are the *Information Please Almanac, Atlas and Yearbook,* begun in 1947 by Dan Golenpaul Associates, and *The Official Associated Press Almanac* which is only five years old and calls itself, correctly, the successor to the *New York Times Encyclopedic Almanac.* The redundancy in titles is *not* helpful because these almanacs are all a potpourri of information and encyclopedic both in theory and practice, are by strict definition "yearbooks," and all have sections with maps which give them the claim to being atlases. This is as true of the *World* as it is of *Information Please* and *Associated Press.* For less than $3.00 each, I recommend that you purchase a new one every few years. Like daily newspapers and network TV evening news programs, these three almanacs are highly imitative of one another and have similar strengths and weaknesses.

The American Almanac, first issued in 1974 (New York: Grosset & Dunlap, Inc.) is a different breed and, except for its paperback ready availability and price ($3.95) puts in the spotlight the fact that 100 percent of United States Government Printing Office publications are in the "public domain" which is to say they are unprotected by copyright law and the authors, who are government employees, secure no royalties. *The American Almanac* does this by simply being a photo-offset of the 94th edition of *The Statistical Abstract of the United States* with short and lively introduction by Ben J. Wattenberg added and a red paper cover wrapped around the whole thing. It is a magnificent source for the very obvious and simple reason that the *Statistical Abstract,* prepared annually by the Bureau of the Census, is a first-class arrangement of all that is officially known through the dedication and skill of public employees over many decades.

Because each Congress runs for two years (94th Congress – elected November, 1974 – functions from January, 1975 through December, 1976), its handbooks are essentially biennial. For instance, an excellent paperback called *The Almanac of American Politics* came out first in 1972 with the "second biennial edition" appearing in 1974. The price moved from $4.95 to $6.95; yet it remains an exceptionally enterprising and valuable reference tool by describing the traits of each state and Congressional district, with profiles of every incumbent, much on primary as well as general elections for each, key votes within Congress and ratings by various groups from left to right. While it possesses a heavy dose of originality, *The Almanac of American Politics* is distinctly derivative from the official *Congressional Directory* which is published new each year for every annual session of each Congress. Thus, *The Almanac of American*

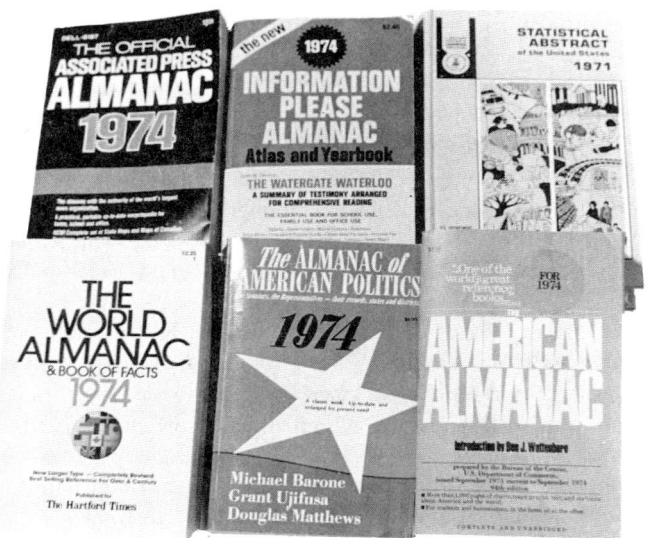

Politics is an overblown title that typifies commercial publishing as it is restricted to Congress and not only omits local politics and state legislative politics but ignores Governors as well. To underline the point, it contains photographs of every member of the House and Senate in Washington, but no Governors.

Speaking of Congress still but of yet another *type* of almanac, there is an example of a retrospective annual volume since 1945, namely the *Congressional Quarterly Almanac.* This expensive tome and its related publications are fully treated in the section on Congressional sources. We pause only to stress that the 1974 volume is actually about that year and is published early in 1975 to assure full coverage of the previous calendar year.

Almanacs may be variously dated and their contents may change much or little from edition to edition, but it is well to have it in mind that almanacs or yearbooks exist for an incalculable number of subjects. Thus there is a biennial *Book of the States,* the *Encyclopedia of Social Work,* the *Municipal Yearbook,* and yearbooks for many encyclopedias. Many directories are packed with useful information. These include the *American Library Directory,* the *United States Government Manual,* as well as the various handbooks of state governments, and the *Catholic Almanac* and the *American Jewish Year Book.*

Bibliography

American Almanac, The. 1974-   New York: Grosset & Dunlap, Inc., 1974-   . The Statistical Abstract of the United States.

American Jewish Year Book. 5660-   . Sept. 5, 1899-   . Phila.: Jewish Pub. Soc., 1899-   . Vol. 1-   . Annual. Beginning with vol. 44, each volume contains an American Jewish bibliography.

Barone, Michael; Ujifusa, Grant; and Matthews, Douglas. *The Almanac of American Politics.* 1972-   . Boston: Gambit, Inc., 1972-   . Second biennial ed., 1974.

Book of the States. Vol. 1, 1935-   . Lexington, Ky: Council of State Governments, 1935-   . Biennial, in even-numbered years. Two supplements issued in odd-numbered years, one listing elective officials and legislation; the other listing administrative officials classified by functions.

Catholic Almanac, 1974. Edited by Felician A. Foy, O.F.M. Huntington, Ind.: Our Sunday Visitor, Inc., 1973. Successor to *National Catholic Almanac.* Annual. Title, imprint and sponsoring body vary.

Encyclopedia of Social Work. Vol. 1, 1929-   . Successor to the *Social Work Yearbook.* New York: National Association of Social Workers. Vol. 15, 1965, edited by Harry L. Lurie. Issued at intervals of five or ten years.

Information Please Almanac, Atlas and Yearbook. 1947-   . Planned and supervised by Dan Golenpaul Associates. New York: Simon & Schuster, 1947-   . Annual. Publisher varies.

Municipal Yearbook, The. Vol. 1, 1934-   . Washington, D.C.: International City Management Association, 1934-   . The authoritative source book of urban data and developments. Annual.

New York Times Encyclopedic Almanac, 1970, The. New York: New York Times Book & Educational Department, 1969. Superseded by the *Official Associated Press Almanac.*

Official Associated Press Almanac, The. 1974-   . Maplewood, N.J.: Hammond Almanac, Inc., 1973. Continues the *New York Times Encyclopedic Almanac.*

U.S. Bureau of the Census. *Statistical Abstract of the United States, The.* Vol. 1, 1878-   . Wash., D.C.: Govt. Prt. Off., 1879-   . Annual.

World Almanac and Book of Facts, The. Vol. 1, 1868-   . New York: Newspaper Enterprise Association, Inc. Annual.

7. Biographies

What, as Harold Lasswell might ask, does a social scientist wish to know about who, why? The pursuit of this question precedes consideration of where and how one is most assuredly to find the answer. Among the ways of dividing this subject of political biography is to consider whether individualized personal information is needed or whether aggregate data are to be assembled.

If the researcher is pursuing facts about an individual, there should be a thoughtful regard for the pertinence of information helpful to understanding.

Simple facts, if sure, are fine for assembling data about a group of people. What was the average age of persons elected to Congress in 1900 as compared to 1970? The *Biographical Directory of the American Congress, 1774-1971,* in a single volume updated every 10 years, will yield the birth dates of practically all these people. It may take so much digging there that the researcher will decide to limit the question to the New York or Illinois delegation, but a simple question can often be answered from one reference book. Bear in mind, however, that birth certificates were not mandatory in most states until the 1890s, so that persons born before then may be unsure of their precise date of birth. Also, many reference books take the subject for granted so that dependence on the subject for information may throw that date and other information off a bit. Thus it was the policy for many years for *Who's Who in America* to permit a woman to make herself younger in this reference book. Certainly, these types of reference books with brief entries about a person are seldom, if ever, given independent checks for accuracy.

A scholarly check is made as a routine matter in the preparation of biographical dictionaries that are posthumous in character. The English *Dictionary of National Biography,* in 21 volumes; the American *Notable American Women, 1607-1950,* in three volumes; the *Dictionary of American Biography,* in 24 volumes up to 1950; and the *Dictionary of Canadian Biography,* for instance, require checks of both birth and death certificates. Quite apart from these sources, which include only persons thought to have had an exceptional impact on their times, the public has been made well aware of the fact that no autopsy was made on Mary Jo Kopechne after her death — evidently of drowning — at Chappaquiddick, Massachusetts during a confused night that continues to have a shrouded effect on the political career of Senator Edward Kennedy. (See Robert Sherrill, "Chappaquiddick Plus Five," *New York Times Magazine,* July 14, 1974, pp. 8-9, 37-38, 44-47.) Mostly, these kinds of facts will not be vital to a political biography, but when they are pertinent it will be important to recognize that and be suspicious about the reliability of the sources.

So far as reference books are concerned, the who's who type — abbreviated lives, self-prepared — and biographical dictionaries — fine, independent-minded, scholarly, posthumous sketches — are sufficiently reliable to do any manner of aggregate study. If one has a list of college presidents, of mayors of New York, of a particular group of judges, top civil servants or leaders in the prohibition, trade union or conservation movements, there are many items of comparable data that can be tracked down through these standard reference sources. For such select populations of ten to 100 people, say, it will be safe, easy and informative to check parental backgrounds, type and amount of formal education, career patterns, geographical associations and so on.

For larger, nameless groups of people, the official censuses of population will be needed. Begin with *The Statistical Abstract of the United States,* published annually since the 1880s, and begin especially with the tables that provide aggregate information. This is the source to learn how many this and how many that: Greeks who came to America between 1911 and 1920; live births per state; years of schooling over the years; and so on. Of course, the *Statistical Abstract* is based upon the various censuses of the Census Bureau, and the sources in the tables of the *Abstract* will lead one on to millions of pages of more raw data about migration, immigration and emigration; about live births and age of death on the average; about ethnic and national origins of much of the American population. But, hark, while the information is presented in stark tables about thousands and millions, it is well to remember the humane basis of the information, which is to say the many lives of quiet desperation that accumulate into these sometimes lifeless and forbidding tables.

One wishes to move back and forth in appreciating the lives of individuals and the cumulative record of the populations of the world. In searching out details about individuals it is likely to be the world famous, the celebrities and infamous figures in the political life. Gerald R. Ford is the 38th President of the United States; William H. Rehnquist is the 110th member of the Supreme Court — which is to say that there is, indeed, a political *elite* to consider. Returning to that political elite we return as well to the question raised at the outset: what details are significant to the researcher?

Who's Who in America promises its "biographees" of eventual immortality in the follow-up reference series called *Who Was Who in America*. Editorial policy for inclusion is particularly generous toward elected officials at every level of American government and, even, includes prominent world figures. There is a strong disposition to include university administrators and professors, even those associated with remote, less known institutions. This no doubt derives from a practice ended in the 1950s of carrying advertisements of colleges. *Who's Who in America* is a relatively poor place to obtain information about other professionals such as lawyers, accountants, advertising people and journalists. Once a biographee is dead, he is so listed and then included in the next compilation of *Who Was*, now issued about every five years. If there is no death notice and the individual passes 100 years and doesn't answer his mail he can look forward assuredly to making *Who Was* anyhow.

The chief advantage of this source in particular and who's who type reference to biography, of which there are a great many, is that they are extraordinarily handy for basic facts for orthodox career people. The information includes birth date and place, names of parents, college degrees, titles of positions held with dates, honors, wife's name and children, along with present business and home addresses. The publisher takes care to double check this with the biographee and there is little doubt that a reliable result ensues in more than 99 per cent of the biographies. But while the character of *Who's Who* insures us solid facts from the careful careerist (Henry Steele Commager offers a four-inch example) who will compulsively proofread every date, degree, and honor, the very reliance on the biographee for information insures that vices and blemishes will be hidden, or at least shielded.

On the cloudy side of the street, therefore, prominent criminals are omitted, for there is no place for achieving Americans like John Dillinger, Charles Manson or James Earl Ray. This is understandable and expected since burglars and murderers often have little claim to fame other than their criminality. But what happens when the mighty fall? In *Who Was Who* James Michael Curley, the Boston politician, is spared mention of his crimes just as the difficulties with the law faced by the financier Samuel Insull are omitted. When he was a fair-haired youthful president of the Carnegie Endowment for Peace in the 1940s, Alger Hiss was included in *Who's Who* (Vol. 25, 1948-49, p. 1141). When tainted as a possible

Communist sympathizer through conviction for perjury, Hiss was dropped altogether. Today, *Who's Who* has more relaxed standards toward the wayward, though not for Hiss who never appears after Volume 25, ironically dropped just as he reached celebrity status. And Whittaker Chambers, author of *Witness,* never made *Who's Who* at all. A public official convicted of crime may or may not remain in *Who's Who*. A person of prominence who is controversial, or simply declines to answer his mail, such as Whittaker Chambers is simply omitted. *Who Was Who* veers from this with sufficient passage of time, notably in its Historical Volume, 1607-1896, which consists of originally researched data compiled in the 1950s. The point is proved by this entry: "James, Jesse Woodson, desperado" which gives a first class account of life and death in who's who style. E. Howard Hunt of Watergate fame is shown in the 1972-73 edition of *Who's Who* with all his marvelous "covers" for his years of work in the Central Intelligence Agency, three pseudonyms for his sideline as an author of fiction, and his office address: "The White House, Washington, DC." Following his conviction of a Federal crime, the 1974-75 edition holds everything in place, adds one pseudonym and shows an address change, though not to the Federal Correctional Institution, Danbury. Agnew, Spiro Theodore retains his full biographical sketch in the 1974-75 edition except for identification as "former vice pres. US," and the fact that this position was "resigned 1973."

The fuller biographical dictionaries, with sketches of two to five full pages and sometimes longer, are much juicier to read and contain information that is independently verified. For the dead, the *Dictionary of American Biography* and the newer *Notable American Women* not only explain falls from grace in some detail but often present psychological theories of an individual's behavior. Though generally laudatory and understanding, these biographies nonetheless go into considerable detail about bad fortune such as with Samuel Insull (1859-1938) in the *DAB*.

The high scholarly quality of the *Dictionary of American Biography* and of *Notable American Women* arises in part from the time lag between a subject's death and the preparation of the sketch. The lapse of time may provide access to manuscripts and other data on the subject not available immediately. There is also time for substantial articles and books written from different vantage points. The slow pace of publication, exasperating as it may sometimes be to readers, provides the authors of these sketches with what Holmes once called the sober second thought. There will be occasions, of course, when nothing short of full-length biographies can serve a researcher in political science, but the short biographies in the *DAB* and *NAW* will often name those longer sources while also providing reliable information and informed interpretations of important figures.

One need not believe that history and politics are exclusively the accumulation of people's lives, or the lives of great people, to accept the idea that individuals make a difference. When Supreme Court decisions are made by five-to-four divisions and a President takes bold action, or fails to, our attention is drawn strongly to the character and personality of individuals. Political scientists are certain to benefit from readings in the *DAB* on Abraham Lincoln by James G. Randall (11:242-259), on Calvin Coolidge by Allan Nevins (Supp. I:191), and on Franklin D. Roosevelt by Frank Friedel (Supp. III:641-667). The essays on jurists, especially those by Felix Frankfurter on O. W. Holmes, Jr. (Supp. I:417-427) and Benjamin Cardozo (Supp. II:93-96) express the author's own views of the Supreme Court's proper function. The original index of the *Dictionary of American Biography* fills all of volume 20 and is remarkable in its detail and usefulness. It must be observed further that many of the essays written in the 1930s have been put in the shade by new information and studies of the subjects so that the *DAB,* like all reference books, must be read with a sense of the date they were prepared. Yet the fullness of sources available on each person is usually outstanding with some two pages of fine print at the end of the essays on Lincoln and F. D. Roosevelt, for example.

Professor Arthur Meier Schlesinger (1888-1965) proposed in 1955 that the need for a biographical dictionary of American women be investigated, and within two years the Advisory Board of the Women's Archives at Radcliffe College committed itself to the preparation of *Notable American Women.* Of the nearly 15,000 individuals included in the *DAB,* only some 700 were women. While only twice that many, 1,337 for the period 1607 to 1950, are included in *Notable American Women,* the essays are splendid probings of the backgrounds, motivations, achievements and significance of each subject. Completed before the contemporary woman's movement, *NAW* is nevertheless the beneficiary of contemporary attitudes and of scholarly standards. *NAW* begins with a comprehensive account of the changing settings in which women found themselves at different stages of American history. ("Introduction" by Janet Wilson James, vol. 1, pp. xvii-l.) Otherwise the apparatus for locating particular persons is left to the alphabet and, unhappily, to a simple classified list of selected biographies at the end of the third and final volume. Here, at least, can be found 54 political figures divided into the categories of advisors and appointees, Congresswomen and Senators, other elected officials, party workers, and propagandists. There is not one of these 54 who are above the level of tertiary importance; indeed, this judgment accords with the view of women as having been notoriously submerged in the years covered. Not that these accounts of politically active women are not interesting, but I have found myself more attracted to the explanations of the lives of women such as Jane Addams by Anne Firor Scott (I:16-22), Mary Baker Eddy, founder of the Church of Christ, Scientist, by Sydney E. Ahlstrom (I:551-561), and of Ida Tarbell, the historian and muckraker, by David M. Chalmers (III:428-431). While many women of special interest are actresses, authors and film stars, there is ample attention to abolitionists, feminists, and reformers in such fields of health, labor and prisons. There are also classifications of Negro women, peace advocates, suffragists and, the only ordained group included by status, the wives of the Presidents.

Biographical references, like all reference books of any durability, have incorporated some formula that makes them commercially successful, and it is often through the scrutiny of that formula that one learns of the book's selection of names, sources of data, thoroughness and accuracy of presentation and usefulness as a tip-off to further information. *Current Biography,* a single fresh volume a year since 1940, affords an excellent example of a durable formula. Published by the H. W. Wilson Company, it is compatible with the *Biography Index* and the dozen or so other indexes to periodicals issued by this firm, compatible commercially because the house must obtain thousands of magazines and journals on a regular basis and has been enterprising in putting these to more than one use. Articles in these magazines and journals are merely categorized and listed in the indexes but in *Current Biography* they are depended upon for informational content. When people such as Ralph Nader, Joan Baez, or Janis Joplin make the news, they are written up in several magazines and become well-known. *Current Biography* editors have an obvious measure of this and soon go to work to write an original sketch of such personalities on this basis. A bibliography at the end of each article tells one where further details will be found. If the personality's star continues to rise it will be important for the researcher to follow up on a dated entry in *Current Biography* by utilizing the *Biography Index,* a great research tool because it lists fresh articles on long-gone people: Dorothea Dix, Tom Mix, Lillian Tish, Dred Scott, Calvin Coolidge and Scott Joplin.

Two further points should be remembered if the research is on a political figure and the interest is in some particular aspect of a career. For theorists like James Madison, John C. Calhoun, Thurmond Arnold, Alexis de Tocqueville or Robert Dahl it will be important to look at their own writings and critiques of their ideas. These will be found through the card catalog and in shorter form in the leading biographical dictionaries and encyclopedias. There are more than 300 biographies in the *International Encyclopedia of the Social Sciences* (those on William Graham Sumner, Machiavelli and Francis Galton are outstanding examples). In addition to the card catalog (where full scale biographies in books will be found) are government publications. Of special interest in this second category is the work of Congressional committees in confirming executive and judicial appointments. Thurgood Marshall, for instance, was confirmed as a Federal appeals judge and as Solicitor General as well as for the Supreme Court, so that three different hearings will be found on him. There are a handful that are unprinted or are so perfunctory that they are useless, but the confirmation hearings of Nelson Rockefeller are published and are, to put it properly, a goldmine of information about the Rockefeller wealth. Much of this gets into the newspapers and magazines, but the published hearings provide a rich source of data on prominent people in two branches of government and are revealing, of course, of the Congressmen who ask the questions. Going further down the road, the death of an individual who is or who was prominent in government will often produce a memorial proceeding, especially in Congress or the Courts. The *Congressional Record* in July, 1974 has profuse tributes and much information about the life of former Senator Wayne Morse, for example, while the *United States Reports* in 1972 contains full obituaries and commentaries on Justices Black and Harlan who died only a few months apart.

In the publishing trade there are but two seasons, fall which runs from summer and peaks before Christmas, and spring which starts in January and runs downhill toward June. In the fall of 1974 two one-volume biographical reference books, prepared months before, hit the bookstores with the embarrassing omission of President Gerald R. Ford. But since everything gets dated sooner or later, this bad luck in a publishing schedule is insufficient ground to condemn the two books which fill a certain void: *Webster's American Biographies* and the *Encyclopedia of American Biography*.

Webster's American Biographies has many faults including the omission of cross-references and of sources about the biographees. It is anti-intellectual in the true sense that "fame" rather than contributions of the mind are the criteria of inclusion. There are many, many athletes, actors and entertainers compared to historians, economists and sociologists. Political scientists are listed in the "Careers and Professions Index" as

64 BIOGRAPHIES

Because the significance of individual personal behavior in politics is so varied and can be so profound, political scientists often need to search for biographical data. This shelf of books are among those of value. (1) The *Biographical Directory of the American Congress* contains formal and succinct summaries of the lives of all members since 1774, updated every ten years. (2) *Who's Who in America* is published biennially. (3) *Who Was Who in America* runs to six volumes with an index in the most recent one. (4) The *Dictionary of American Biography (DAB)* has 24 volumes of interpretive sketches of prominent figures whose deaths fell before 1951. New volumes will be added. (5) *Notable American Women (NAW)*, now in paperback, just three volumes in total, is wonderful reading. (6) *Current Biography* contains composite journalistic accounts of individuals at their point of emergence into public view. (7) *Biography Index* can help find more on the famous and something about the obscure. (8) *Webster's American Biographies* and (9) *Encyclopedia of American Biography* are one-volume collections of sketches of household names, each imperfect but worthwhile. (10) *The New York Times Obituaries Index* is good if the newspaper itself is available; otherwise forget it.

historians and those included contain only the blandest descriptive phrases of their significance. Thus Hannah Arendt's "penetrating analysis of history and of political man" contain a "strain of pessimism." After Zechariah Chaffe's book *Freedom of Speech* was published in 1920, "he very quickly became recognized as a leading thinker on the subject of civil liberties." Edward S. Corwin "produced a large number of penetrating and widely influential studies." These are listed but we learn nothing of his cast of mind, his policy preferences, and just who was influenced in what way by reading his books. Of Harold Lasswell's life we learn nothing intellectual but only that he "wrote over the years a large number of influential works on a wide range of subjects in his field" and, to boot, "a number of important papers." We are told that Lasswell made a big contribution by developing the notion of "policy science" which is defined as "an amalgam of law, political science, sociology, and psychology into one great overarching discipline dealing with the general subject of public choice and decision making." Nearly every lawyer ever to be on the Supreme Court, hundreds of Congressmen and all Presidents but Ford are included, and the articles are competently written and factually sound. There seems to be a special problem here that stems from the complete absence of sources on the individual subjects treated. This failure suggests that existing biographical sources were pressed into service in a hit-or-miss way. Of course I have already learned a good deal from this volume and am even grateful for the brief recital of Herbert Putnam's good works as Librarian of Congress which I had not previous appreciated. But really this "useful" biographical dictionary is a caricature of scholarship. Merriam-Webster knew that people like me and libraries all over would buy this and they were correct.

The *Encyclopedia of American Biography* might properly describe the full decennial census, but here it is smugly used as a title of a one-volume collection of quickie biographies of slightly more than one thousand (1,000) Americans from colonial times to the present. John Garraty has written a graceful introduction justifying the choice of subjects that is commendable. But there is no index of any kind and there is no characterization of the authors of the sketches although some are recognized authorities. Each biography is in two parts, the first of which "attempts to be completely objective" by providing the rock-bottom essentials about the subject's life. "The second part of each entry attempts," according to Garraty, "to evaluate the total career of the subject."

Most of the entries are so brief, and often so one-sided, that the worthy goal of providing interpretation is severely undercut. Thus Bernard Baruch

(1870-1965), the financier and self-styled "adviser to Presidents," is lauded for his good works, patriotism and shrewdness in an appraisal by Margaret L. Coit. As in almost all entries, Coit cites only one source — in this instance her own biography of Baruch. It is hardly surprising that she would omit an alternative interpretation of Baruch's character and career set forth by Alexander M. Bickel in a withering review of her book in the *Yale Law Journal* (67:519, January 1958). Many other evaluations of the careers of their subjects are entirely saccharine such as ones of Irving Babbitt (1865-1933) by his admirer Russell Kirk ignoring the critical view of David Spitz in his *Patterns of Anti-Democratic Thought* (Macmillan, 1949). Called a philosopher in the *EAB*, Babbitt is not mentioned in the recent *Encyclopedia of Philosophy*. That Kingman Brewster, President of Yale is a great educational leader, among the 1,000 most notable Americans, goes unquestioned.

On the other side of the ledger is such a vicious attack on Spiro T. Agnew, in eleven sentences by the editor Garraty himself, as to suppose that no one ever before has or ever in the future may bring such disgrace to himself. It is a fashionably liberal statement of outrage. But within this contemptuous diagnosis lurk assumptions that deserve attention: Is it the function of the President and Vice-President "to unify the country" or, as products of the party system, should they not stand for something? Did the original nomination of Agnew show that the convention nominating practices are inherently dangerous? The Theodore Roosevelt and Harry Truman examples are often cited to support the contrary view, and the alternative scrutiny under the 25th Amendment suggests that the ideal still eludes us. The discussion of Agnew's hypocrisy also raises doubts, especially about liberals who urge integration in the public schools while sending their own children to private institutions aloof from community tensions. There is no mention of hypocrisy by "limosine liberals," discussed by Safire in the *New Language of Politics*. Yet the *EAB* does provide a corrective to the listing of Agnew in *Who's Who in America*. For other, fuller and more balanced judgments about Spiro Agnew, see the 54 newspaper reactions at the time of his resignation in *Editorials on File* for 1973, pages 1274-1293.

A parting word. For facts about Plato, Aristotle, St. Thomas, Joan of Arc and others, see *Webster's Biographical Dictionary* (obsessed as I am with Whittaker Chambers and Alger Hiss, it must be recorded that neither is included here although there are "more than 40,000 concise biographies of famous people" included), *Atlantic Brief Lives* encyclopedia or other standard sources. For the fullest accounts of recently deceased persons like Charles A. Lindbergh, whose career was remarkably political, see the *New York Times* on the day after his death. A special key to obituaries in the *Times* is the one-volume, black covered *New York Times Obituaries Index, 1858-1968.*

Bibliography

Altlantic Brief Lives: A Biographical Companion to the Arts. Edited by Louis Kronenberger. Boston: Little, Brown and Co., 1971. An Atlantic Monthly Press Book.

Biography Index. Vol. 1, 1947-   . New York: H.W. Wilson Co., 1947-   . Cumulative index to biographical material in books and magazines. Quarterly.

Current Biography. Vol. 1, 1940-   . New York: H. W. Wilson Co. Monthly with bound annual cumulations.

Dictionary of American Biography. 20 vols. Pub. under auspices of the American Council of Learned Societies. New York: Charles Scribner's Sons, 1936. Four supplements. Supp. #4, covering 1946-1950, edited by John A. Garraty, 1974.

Dictionary of Canadian Biography. Toronto: Univ of Toronto Press. Vol. 1, 1000-1700 (1966); vol. 2, 1701-1740 (1969); vol. 3, 1741-1770 (1974); vol. 10, 1871-1880 (1972).

Dictionary of National Biography. Founded in 1882 by George Smith. Edited by Leslie Stephen and Sidney Lee. 21 vols. From earliest times to 1900. London: Oxford Univ. Press, 1937-1938. Seven supplements. Supp. #7, covering 1951-1960 with Index for 1901-1960, edited by E. T. Williams and Helen M. Parker, 1971.

Encyclopedia of American Biography. Edited by John A. Garraty and Jerome L. Sternstein. New York: Harper & Row, 1974.

New York Times Obituaries Index, 1858-1968. New York: New York Times, 1970.

Notable American Women, 1607-1950: A Biographical Dictionary. 3 vols. Edited by Edward T. James and Janet W. James. Cambridge, Mass.: Harvard University Press, Belknap Press, 1971.

U.S. Bureau of the Census. *Statistical Abstract of the United States, The.* Vol. 1, 1878-   . Wash. D.C.: Govt. Prt. Off., 1879-   . Annual.

U.S. Congress. *Biographical Directory of the American Congress, 1774-1971.* 11th ed. Wash.: Govt Prt. Off., 1971. 1st ed., 1859.

Webster's American Biographies. Edited by Charles Van Doren and Robert McHenry. Springfield, Mass.: G. & C. Merriam Co., 1974.

BIOGRAPHIES

Webster's Biographical Dictionary: A Dictionary of Names of Noteworthy Persons, with Pronunciations and Concise Biographies. Rev. ed. Springfield, Mass.: G. & C. Merriam Co., 1962. 1st ed., 1943.

Who Was Who in America. Chicago: Marquis-Who's Who, Inc. 6 vols. Historical Volume, 1607-1896; Vol. 1, 1897-1942; Vol. 2, 1943-1950; Vol. 3, 1951-1960; Vol. 4, 1961-1968; Vol. 5, 1969-1973.

Who's Who in America: A Biographical Dictionary of Notable Living Men and Women. 1899- . Chicago: Marquis Who's Who, Inc., 1899- 38th ed., 1974-1975, in 2 vols. Biennial.

8. Political Dictionaries

The list of political and political science dictionaries printed here (full citations will be found in bibliography) are dissected in order to generate in readers' minds the importance of words to students of politics. These specialized, modest books have the character of indispensability of the leading standard dictionaries, however. The differences between the two types should be clear at the outset.

For simple, straight-forward contemporary definitions of words a standard desk dictionary will suffice. None is recommended over another here but *Webster's New Collegiate Dictionary* (1973) having 150,000 entries with 27,000 usage examples is representative of the type. This is based on a second kind of general dictionary, the single-volume "unabridged" *Webster's Third New International Dictionary* (1969) with 450,000 entries and 200,000 usage examples. While this pretends to be the whole thing there is, in truth, a third and fuller type of general dictionary, the type based on the historical record of the evolution in the usage of a word. The greatest of these in this language is the thirteen volume *Oxford English Dictionary* (1933). Using assembly line methods, this great set is now being updated and volume one of *A Supplement to the Oxford English Dictionary,* A-G (1972) is a delight. No other dictionary in English that I have seen gives a political definition for the word "Byzantine" although that connotation has been used by Washington correspondents for years. Evans and Novak wrote of the "Byzantine gamesmanship" in Washington ("Jerry Ford's Friend Mel Laird," *New York,* Sept. 2, 1974, p. 35) and their meaning is clear from the *OED* supplement where Byzantine is defined: "Also, reminiscent of the manner, style, or spirit of Byzantine politics. Hence, intricate, complicated; inflexible, rigid, unyielding." The usage examples are ordered chronologically, the first being from Koestler's *1937 Spanish Testament:* "In the old days people often smiled at the Byzantine structure of the Spanish Army."

While examples of the three types of general dictionaries abound and should really be found in any library, public or private, of any size, the political dictionaries are not indispensable. For one thing, new ones come out every year so that by 1980 there will be another batch of 25 likely, in most cases, to have the same traits to be pointed out here. At the same time it is hoped this critique will have some effect on dictionary makers as well as upon users.

The largest of the volumes reviewed here has fewer than 4,100 entries, and most have far fewer, so that the books are not comprehensive in the sense of exhausting their subject and capturing all possible terminology. It remains true that the more specialized books here, limited to definite subjects, provide cohesive and ample treatments. This is particularly true for Abrams on cities, Luttwak on armaments, and Safire on American political catchwords and usages. They are really books that could have been cast in other forms than dictionaries, but their authors simply found it attractive to do their work in this format rather than as one-act plays or videotape quiz shows. Theirs was an artistic judgment. Having chosen the dictionary form, they then "do their own thing" with it. They cover many more works and subjects than indicated by a count of the entries because they go into so much more depth than the ordinary dictionary attempts. The resulting art form is really different from a dictionary, and as such it seems to me to succeed when it is handled both with imagination and competence. It fails when taken too literally and given insufficient infusions of fresh air and individuality.

Their publishers have doubtless come to believe that acquisition librarians are more likely to give the nod to a book that purports to be a dictionary than a book cast in the form of numbered chapters. Although all of the books here deal with concerns of substantial interest to political scientists, they have little else in common aside from their alphabetical organization.

The editorial apparatus in these dictionaries affords some measure of editorial patience, thoughtfulness, and sophistication. The preliminaries of a preface or foreword and an introduction explain the editorial purpose and plan and, where missing, forecast trouble ahead in the text. Cross-references must be built into the text itself. This feature is absent only in Dunner, an omission explained possibly by the book's being a compilation of entries written by about 200 different political scientists; these authors were not able to refer to each other, and this deficiency was not remedied by the editors. Discussion of method and of sources usually appears in the back matter, along with an index. A judgment of the quality of each apparatus contributes silently to the rating for editing of each dictionary. (Political Dictionaries Exhibit No 1.) It should only be added that the Cranston and Lakoff *Glossary of Political Ideas* deals with such a small number of topics as to obviate the need for complex editorial tools.

By the same token explanatory features become all the more essential as the entries rise to more than 1,000 for Laqueur and for Plano and Greenberg; to nearly 3,000 for Dunner; and to 4,000 in Smith and Zurcher. From all of this it must not be assumed that the apparatus provided tells the full story of quality; it just gives a hint.

The author of a monograph will ordinarily take some pains defining old words and introducing new ones with careful attention to meaning. Good books are strewn with definitions and explanations of words. By this measure many books could be dictionaries and vice versa. It is quite easy to imagine Abrams, Laqueur, Luttwak, or Safire presenting their ideas in other than alphabetical order. Abrams's book is about the impact of various public policies on the economic and social life of cities around the world. Laqueur's book is about the course of ideological conflict among nations since the Russian Revolution with particular attention to the political leaders embroiled. Luttwak concentrates on national rivalries almost exclusively and assesses power capability at strategic rather than tactical levels. Safire has really written a history of the place of charismatic personalities in the communications network of American political life.

Individuals who write dictionaries often do so with some passion, and this is most evident in the works here of Abrams, Laqueur, Luttwak, and Safire. They bring an enthusiasm to their work in the tradition of Samuel Johnson and Henry L. Mencken. Abrams's book will be a joy to students because the brief definitions of "land fragmentation," "noise," "physiographic determination," and "piece of the action" are accompanied by apt historical information and pungent editorialization. The first of these, among his shorter entries, shows how Abrams brings history and current issues together and includes a typical array of cross references. Cities are ancient and exist all over the world, and it is fitting that Abrams's cosmopolitan learning cheerfully registers in this book. He infuses it with humanizing references and with incisive explanations of the consequences of "blockbusting" and the "industrial-development bond." Abrams has prepared a highly personal tour of the urban world from the experience of a man who was at once a lawyer, a political figure, and a careful reader in the literature of city planning, law, history and the social sciences. Abrams commands the respect and gratitude of all who seek to know this vast subject.

Laqueur's *A Dictionary of Politics* arranges itself through cross-references around the great ideological struggles of the past forty years. These are not explicitly suggested but close study shows this to be a highly integrated book. *On Fascism:* Mussolini, Ethiopia, Nazi Party, *Mein Kampf,* Hitler, Concordat, Goebbels, Goering, Munich, Chamberlain,

The word explosion in political life and in the disciplined study of political science is registered in these 10 single-volume, special dictionaries. Similar ones appear all the time. While these can be helpful, often very much so, it is wise at times to turn to general dictionaries. These should include hand dictionaries as well as the great *Oxford English Dictionary (OED)* and American unabridged dictionaries.

Political Dictionaries

Exhibit No. 1

EDITORIAL APPARATUS IN SELECTED POLITICAL DICTIONARIES

	Total Entries	Preface or Introduction	Method Essay	Essay on Sources	Index	Cross References	Editorial Ranking
Abrams, *Language of Cities*	979	+	+	+	+	+	2
Cranston & Lakoff, *Glossary of Political Ideas*	52	+	–	+	–	+	5
Dunner, *Dictionary of Political Science*	2768	+	+	–	–	–	9
Elliott, *Dictionary of Politics*	952	–	–	–	–	+	10
Laqueur, *Dictionary of Politics*	1433	+	–	–	–	+	7
Luttwak, *Dictionary of Modern War*	539	+	+	+	–	+	4
Plano & Greenberg, *American Political Dictionary*	1143	+	+	–	+	+	3
Roberts, *Dictionary of Political Analysis*	477	+	+	–	–	+	6
Safire, *New Language of Politics*	845	+	+	+	+	+	1
Smith and Zurcher, *Dictionary of American Politics*	4080	+	–	–	–	+	8

DICTIONARIES 73

Mosley, Gestapo, Crystal Night, Spanish Civil War, Himmler, Concentration Camps, Holocaust, Eichmann, Churchill, Pearl Harbor, Roosevelt, Axis Powers, Japan, World War II, and Nuremberg War Crime Trials, among others. *On Communism:* Bolshevism, USSR, Lenin's Testament, World Communism, Sovietisation, Purges, Moscow Trials, Show Trials, Slave Labor, Pyatakov, Kaganovich, Khrushchev, Tito, Yugoslavia, Czechoslovakia, Kuomintang, Mao Tse-tung, Chinese People's Republic, Sino-Soviet Conflict, Lin Piao. Similar strings of entries spell out the development of American Policy, Zionism and the Arab response; Colonialism and the Third World; tensions in East Europe; and conflict over the unification of Europe. Laqueur says a good deal, too, on the theme that domestic politics affects foreign policy. This is particularly evident in the treatment of several personalities, institutions and incidents in the domestic political life of France and the United States.

Luttwak, Deputy Director of the Middle East Study Group in Jerusalem, brings an impressive intellect and a strong interest in specifics to the universe of modern war and weaponry. His essay on "war" is a concise philosophical statement about the four rival concepts, hardly precise parallel categories, of von Clausewitz, Marxist-Leninists, pacifists, and peace-researchers. This discussion leads into "total war," "central war," "deterrence," "controlled response," "propaganda," and "political warfare." There are also many articles on particular international incidents or events such as "Warsaw Pact." But the passion shows itself in the fastidiousness of detail in the more technical articles. A book like this relies on other sources, and Luttwak's excellence is rooted in his skeptical, intelligent handling of those sources. Thus he observes that *JANE'S All the World's Aircraft* and related reference sources do not assess the claims of manufacturers. He praises the timeliness of another reference source, *The Military Balance,* issued annually by the Institute for Strategic Studies in London. Luttwak's feeling for words is expressed in his foreword:

> For obvious reasons, there is a shortage of reliable information about the more advanced weapons. The Russians publish almost nothing, and while Western arms' manufacturers do publish a great deal, many of them also cultivate 'brochuremanship', where extravagant claims are camouflaged under the pseudo-technical language fashionable in military circles.('Advanced' means that it does not work yet; 'semi-automatic' means that everything has to be done by hand; 'anti-tank secondary kill capability' means that only a hero or a fool would approach a real-life tank armed with one of those...) Information about Soviet weapons comes almost

entirely from intelligence reports which are leaked, selectively, by the Western military. See *Scarp* for a Soviet I C B M whose performance details were published when the Pentagon had to prod a reluctant Congress to release funds for the *Safeguard* missile defence system.

Luttwak explains that modern weapons have longer lives than is generally thought, and this assertion is proved convincingly in the entry for "B-52" which is cross-referenced to "stratofortress" used in the December 1972 bombing of Hanoi and Haiphong. Detailed specifications of size, range, cost, numbers, load, and so on are included for this and other weapons.

Safire's dictionary treats everything in sight with generosity. His accurate subtitle calls the book *A Dictionary of Catchwords, Slogans & Political Usage,* and a long introductory essay and final note on sources and research, plus a bibliography and index to names, make the book a pleasure to read as well as a durable reference. The index to names converts this into an excellent book of quotations, one that remedies omission from *Bartlett's Quotations* of notable *political* sayings. Innumerable entries give a history that reaches out with a cascade of observations as, for example, with "MY FRIENDS" which starts with FDR, shows that Horatio Seymour used the greeting in 1863, and unwinds with a discussion of the subject of salutations generally, with references to John Witherspoon, Napoleon, Chief Tecumseh, Jefferson, Taft, Kennedy, Truman and Willkie. This entry concludes with details about Roosevelt's apocryphal "Fellow immigrants" address to the Daughters of the American Revolution, April 21, 1938, where the President simply said: "Remember, remember always, that all of us, and you and I especially, are descended from immigrants and revolutionists." There are entries for "LIMOUSINE LIBERAL," "MANIFEST DESTINY," "MEDICARE," "MILITARY-INDUSTRIAL COMPLEX," "MOONLIGHTING," "ONE MAN, ONE VOTE," "RIGHT TO KNOW," "PORK BARREL" and "POTOMAC FEVER." The book is written by a journalist for readers interested in the development of American political jargon. It is not a political science or an academic book. It is to be highly recommended for its thoroughness, the detail with which entries have been researched and the generous way in which a coinage is turned around prismatically for examination.

Its title to the contrary, Florence Elliott's book is of relatively little interest or value to students of politics. In saying Lyndon B. Johnson "did not contest the elections of November 1968," the author treats us to a correct statement that is an inadequate reading of the truth. In a curious gratuity Elliott gives Harry S. Truman a middle name, Swinomish, when he had none. This dictionary seldom touches political terms and does not tell what precisely is political about its entries on individuals, nations, and events. Its discussions of "League of Nations," "Luxemburg," and "Mendès-France" are barely more than what a fair world almanac would provide. Elliott and Laqueur use the identical title, *A Dictionary of Politics,* and both books are intended to cover the same nations, institutions, ideologies, conflicts and personages in the recent past. Both have an English or European vantage point. Here the similarity ends, simply because Laqueur is interpretive and Elliott is not. Elliott's book in effect is a rather poor World Almanac for 1968-69, and is is simply audacious commercialism that it should be portrayed as *A Dictionary of Politics.*

A Glossary of Political Ideas is a collection of terse essays by fourteen British social scientists edited by Maurice Cranston and here edited with additions for American readers by Sanford A. Lakoff. The first of fifty-two entries are "Anarchism," "Authority," "Coexistence," "Colonialism," "The Common Good," "Communism," and "Conservatism." The treatment is in the conventional mode of classical political philosophy with "Equality" never reaching the twentieth century. Yet the book includes brief entries for "Titoism" too sparse to be useful and one for "Trade Unionism" that is too British to be of any service to a student of American institutions. There is a bibliography following each entry. It isn't at all clear what this book is intended for. The entries are less complete than those on nearly every similar topic in the *International Encyclopedia of the Social Sciences,* and of the newer four-volume *Dictionary of the History of Ideas.* There is not enough space available for an author to get off the ground. The result is a book of marginal value to a student beginning to think about the great subjects of political philosophy and of even less interest to a well-read scholar. This Cranston and Lakoff dictionary is competent and reliable, in contrast to Elliott, but it is not imaginatively conceived or energetically executed.

The three dictionaries by Dunner, by Plano and Greenberg, and by Smith and Zurcher have value for the audience of beginning students whose political memories barely reach back to the assassination of President Kennedy. There are hundreds of words that apply to some event or some recurrent matter in the history of American politics. It is a conceit of age to note rudely youth's ignorance of Joe McCarthy's "point of order" or of the 1952 Eisenhower delegates' "fair play amendment." These books will surely instruct undergraduate students of American government and politics. They simply cannot be endorsed as the kind of quality political dictionary graduate and other professional students of politics should use.

The Dunner dictionary is the work of many hands, with very brief entries for its many items about world and American history and politics. It is concerned with events of the early years of the Republic as much as it is of recent matters. Except for a worthwhile introductory essay on political science by Dunner, there is very little social science in the book. It does contain longer and better entries for the same items than will be found in Smith and Zurcher. Dunner is also distinguished by its many brief biographies.

Biographical entries appear in three of the political dictionaries but not in the other seven. (Political Dictionaries Exhibit No. 2.) Those in Laqueur are ably researched and written to stress the political significance of the personages described. Those in Dunner contain greater biographical detail, are more concise and often capture in just a few words the key point about an individual. The biographical portraits in Elliott are weakly drawn and omit vital details as well. Mostly, all of these entries are inferior to the short biographies in the *New Columbia Encyclopedia.* In other words, they may jog one's memory in an emergency, if they are handy, but the biographical entries in these dictionaries are not to be substituted for a quick piece of library research. On the positive side, biographical entries inform us that human beings coin political words and develop political ideas as well as act in political life. The inclusion of biographies reduces the function of these dictionaries for the exacting work of word definition and fails, partly by attempting too much that is diversionary.

Political Dictionaries

Exhibit No. 2

POLITICAL DICTIONARIES WITH BIOGRAPHICAL ENTRIES

Editor and Title	Total Entries	Total Biographies	Per Cent Biographies
Dunner, *Dictionary of Political Science*	2768	549	20
Elliott, *A Dictionary of Politics*	952	140	15
Laqueur, *A Dictionary of Politics*	1433	454	32

Plano and Greenberg have selected 1143 terms, agencies, court decisions, and statutes "for their pertinency to the general introductory course in Americal government and to an understanding of comtemporary political events." (Preface, p. v.) A strong topical ordering gives this book the flavor of a basic text rather than a mere companion. As such, the authors provide no explicit story line but present a bland system of government with few rifts. Societal traits and tensions are ignored, and the tour of Federal agencies is comparable but far less comprehensive than that provided by the *United States Government Manual.* The entries in a chapter titled "political ideas" barely carry the subject into the twentieth century which is to say that there is essentially nothing of the bahavioral persuasion in political science in this book. The comments on "ideology" and "pluralism" give no hint of the disputations in the discipline over the proper application and utility of such terms. The book becomes a catalog of familiar enough terms, informing or reminding the nonspecialist about the *Wong Kim Ark* case, the Ramspeck Act and the Hare Plan. Like many books with technical inadequacies, this dictionary does not point the reader beyond itself; it gives citations to court cases but not to statutes and rarely tells where the information presented in each entry came from or where one can look further.

The fault of all three of the dictionaries of American government is not their limited size but in the way items are treated. Not only the words included in these dictionaries but also the omissions betray the absence of a sense of history, of a theory of political power and development, and of an attendant concern for exactness. That government contractors have special legally-imposed obligations could not be learned here. Yet, long before 1965 when "affirmative action" was coined to expand employment pools to hire without regard to race or sex, the Federal government was using its contracts to dictate wages, hours, loyalty standards, and other employment policies to numerous corporations.

Although Roberts's ideal is more precise usage, his *Dictionary of Political Analysis* is offered as "a mirror of the present vocabulary of the discipline, not a proposal for a future technical word list from which all ambiguities and imprecisions have been removed" (Introduction, p.xx). There is much more here than words of political analysis such as "model" and "attitude scaling": as the book treats "Zionism" and many other political movements as well. It is notably weak in entries on American political institutions.

Roberts does make an admirable start in introducing the subject of contemporary political science in dictionary form. He includes "gatekeepers" and refers the reader ahead to "systems analysis," which is discussed in a brief essay. The right distinction is drawn between "paradigm" and "ideal type." There is a good definition of "interest articulation" and the only adequate mention of "community studies" in any of these dictionaries. Political scientists wishing to catch up to the growth of the behavorial persuasion might use Roberts's book as a Berlitz guide to "cohort analysis," "computer utilisation," "conversion process," "Delphi method," "droop quota," "funnel of causality," "grounded theory," "ladder values," "longitudinal studies," "macro-politics," "meta-policy," "Pareto optimum," "pillarisation," "psephology," "reductionist theories," and "teleological explanation." Many of Roberts's entries are a page or two long, and practically all have cross-references. The best entries contain citations that take the right path as far as they go. Books in point are mentioned but page numbers and journal articles are lacking.

Having carped at some authors for neglecting the discipline of political science, I must fault Roberts for inadequate handling of established legal and political usage. "Conspiracy," "sedition," and "civil rights" might just as well be omitted as given such cursory treatment. They are not words of political analysis in any event, and their meanings in different times and places give them none of the traits possessed by such terms as "attitude scaling." The political scientist as historian and observer of the passing parade will inform himself of the British Secrets Act and of "shield laws," but the kind of dictionary Roberts provides will not carry him far. The political scientist as analyst, on the other hand, has an entirely different intellectual need which Roberts seeks to serve.

As a literary genre, the dictionary of politics is largely uninterested in the history of the words it treats. In his final book (*Two Hundred Million Americans in Search of a Government,* p. 14), E. E. Schattschneider asserted that political science was impossible a century ago because its vocabulary was inadequate. We have had to borrow. He showed as convincingly as anyone could that the words of politics are derivative, most being old words which have acquired new meanings. Schattschneider asked:

> Where do the new words come from? They come from everywhere. Some are figures of speech, as machine, ring, heckle. Some are derived from the place in which activities are carried on, as cabinet, house, or lobby, or from a seating arrangement, as left and right. Some come from the church: hierarchy and propaganda. Many come from military life: campaign, filibuster, insurgent, picket and partisan. A host of political words are made by adding a

new ending to an old word: anarchy becomes anarchism, isolate changes to isolationism, nation to nationalism, total to totalitarianism, and so on.

The common words that have acquired special meaning through political usage present one difficulty. But the derivations of words peculiar to political science require careful analysis and attention to give us a clear measure of their meaning. However well-versed in contemporary political science, these lexicographers, save for Roberts, are not dependable teachers of this subject. If they were, they would have done a number of things. First, they would have had to ascertain the universe of publications in which to search for words. The word list need not be comprehensive; seasoned judgment in building a list would be quite acceptable. But one would hope for a careful scanning of, say, the leading texts in the subfields of political science; the leading articles such as those in the Bobbs-Merrill Reprint Series; a checklist of classics and key monographs; and the suggestions of a band of specialists with varied orientations and political dispositions. If there is to be a new wave of dictionaries of political science which inform us all and build upon each other, it will be essential that the sources scoured for words be named.

Second, the words must be defined in context and their history indicated so that their functional and operational meaning can be grasped by the novice.

Third, in reaching out our hypothetical dictionary maker would have cosmopolitan tastes and unbounded curiosity. Not one of these ten dictionaries mentions "true believer" from Eric Hoffer's book of the same title. (Speaking of the active, revivalist phase of mass movements, Hoffer states that this phase is dominated by the "true believer" defined as "the man of fanatical faith who is ready to sacrifice his life for a holy cause." Eric Hoffer, *The True Believer*, p. 10). This is indicative of a too-narrow preoccupation with the words of formal government and the language of dues-paying political scientists.

Fourth, both jargon and humble usages, which are part of the speech of political scientists who forget or never knew where the words came from, could be captured in a carefully done dictionary. Remember V. O. Key's "friends and neighbors" in his treatment of Alabama politics? (The "friends and neighbors effect" is Key's phrase for a powerful localism in Alabama factionalism where "candidates for state office tend to poll overwhelming majorities in their home counties and to draw heavy support in adjacent counties." Key believes this "points to the absence of stable, well-organized, state-wide factions of like-minded citizens formed to advocate measures of common concern." V. O. Key, *Southern Politics in*

State and Nation, p. 37.) Other words include "polyarchy" made famous by Robert Dahl. (The idea of employing the word "democracy" to connote the ideal and "polyarchy" the real, the latter to serve as a measure of achieving the former appears first in Robert A. Dahl and Charles E. Lindblom, *Politics, Economics, and Welfare,* pp. 272-323. Dahl has reintroduced "polyarchy" instead of the word "pluralism" in the latest edition of his text, Robert A. Dahl, *Democracy in the United States,* p. vii.)

Fifth, we need rival definitions of our most used words such as political parties. The first thing to say about "political party" surely is that the most thoughtful students of the subject prefer differing definitions. Alex Gottfried in Dunner comes closest to saying this by quoting Edmund Burke but without a reference or date. He then gives an alternative. But why turn to a political dictionary when a textbook does the job better?

The heaviest borrowing by the dictionaries on American government and political science is from law, and a consistent deficiency is the absence of key words and the scant interest in the functional meaning of the words that are chosen. Plano and Greenberg are clearly superior in explaining that the Supreme Court controls its business by handling "certiorari" and that interest groups present their views there as "amici curiae." Dunner and Smith and Zurcher include these words but give wooden definitions. None but Smith and Zurcher mention the "removal" of cases from state to Federal courts, but even they neglect to explain its origin in the Judiciary Act of 1789 and its use by the modern civil rights movement. All omit "barratry," the ancient word for soliciting litigation, and consequently cannot discuss the state legislation against barratry designed to stop NAACP lawyers in the South.

If the language of law and politics of an earlier day is not always captured in crisp definitions, there is also failure in handling modern legal usage. There are important lapses in what is included, and because it is unclear what sources are utilized both for the word list and for definitions, the failure sometimes becomes a disaster.

Students of the American constitutional system will find two dictionaries superior in several respects. Plano and Greenberg have divided the material into eighteen topical chapters with the index serving as a full alphabetical guide to entries. The topics are ordered to follow the structure of most textbooks in American government and each entry is composed of two paragraphs, one definitional and the other addressing itself to the significance of the term. This shows relationships well and means that one may profitably, and with a minimum of confusion, actually read the dictionary straight through. Also, important agencies' cases are grouped together toward the end of each chapter, then important cases and important statutes. The new, third edition of Plano and Greenberg offers readers the advantage of up-to-date information about modifications in Supreme Court rulings, especially compared with rival dictionaries. Smith and Zurcher is the only other dictionary that gives much attention to cases and statutes, with Dunner a weak third. (Political Dictionaries Exhibit No. 3) Smith and Zurcher provide short treatments, but reliable ones, of the cases and statutes treated. They also include the specific dates of statutes but neither they, nor Plano and Greenberg, cite statutes either to the *Statutes at Large* or the *United States Code* while both are predictably fastidious to cite cases to the *United States Reports*.

Commentary about political science and political words will help would-be lexicographers prepare better dictionaries. Examples abound in a book of readings edited by Max J. Skidmore offering some forty essays on rhetoric and politics which begin with George Orwell's "Politics and the

Political Dictionaries

Exhibit No. 3

STATUTES AND COURT CASES IN SELECTED POLITICAL DICTIONARIES

Editor and Title	Total Entries	Statutes	Court Cases	Total Statutes & Cases	Per cent of Statutes & Cases
Dunner, *Dictionary of Political Science*	2768	34	23	57	2
Plano and Greenberg, *The American Political Dictionary*	1143	58	105	163	14
Smith and Zurcher, *Dictionary of American Politics*	4080	199	234	433	11

English Language." Skidmore makes many points about the rise and fall of political words that show erosion in the English language that had better keep us from joking about the vain attempts of L'académie Francaise to shore up the language of the French. He argues that it is "no longer possible accurately to grasp any sense of meaning from the words 'defense,' 'victory,' 'free world,' 'aggression,' 'national security,' 'patriotism,' 'policy action,' 'pacification,' 'demilitarized,' and even 'orderly withdrawal.'" (Max J. Skidmore, ed., *Word Politics,* p. 7.) Evidently we must choose between Luttwak's belief that everyone knows what "aggression" means and Skidmore's conclusion that nobody knows. The readings are almost all recent, since 1960, and consequently concern the Vietnam war and the prose of Richard Nixon. But there is debate here, as seen in the attack on Martin Luther King's view of war casualties by Ernest W. Lefever and responses to this criticism. There are fine retrospective articles on what happened to the meaning of words in Nazi Germany which imply that cataclysmic politics foster rapid deterioration of language. By reflecting on political words, rather than defining them, Skidmore's book is more stimulating and may be as useful to political scientists and their students as some political dictionaries.

Political scientists do not yet have a dictionary of professional quality. Most efforts are directed toward undergraduates or the general public. To say that the state of a discipline is revealed by textbooks and reference books is probably to claim too much. Monographs and journal articles surely lead the way. It is a misfortune that the dictionaries in political science seldom incorporate the professional findings. The third type of general dictionary as set forth in *A Dictionary of Americans on Historical Principles* is an excellent example, along with the *OED,* of what is needed in political science. There one will find countless political words like "Jim Crow," "filibuster" and "pork" excellently defined with usage examples cited to the *Congressional Globe* and *Congressional Record* and to obscure American newspapers and books as well.

Bibliography

Abrams, Charles. *The Language of Cities: A Glossary of Terms.* New York: Viking Press, 1971.
Cranston, Maurice, and Lakoff, Sanford A., eds. *A Glossary of Political Ideas.* New York: Basic Books, 1969.
Dahl, Robert A. *Democracy in the United States: Promise and Performance.* 2d ed. Chicago: Rand McNally and Co., 1972.

Dahl, Robert A., and Lindblom, Charles E. *Politics, Economics, and Welfare: Planning and Politico-Economic Systems Resolved into Basic Social Processes.* New York: Harper & Row, 1953.

Dictionary of the History of Ideas. Editor in chief, Philip P. Wiener. 4 vols. New York: Charles Scribner's Sons, 1973.

Dunner, Joseph, ed. *Dictionary of Political Science.* Totowa, N.J.: Littlefield, Adams & Co., 1970.

Elliott, Florence. *A Dictionary of Politics.* 6th ed. Baltimore: Penguin Books, 1969.

Hoffer, Eric. *The True Believer: Thoughts on the Nature of Mass Movements.* New York: Harper and Brothers, 1951.

Key, V. O. *Southern Politics in State and Nation.* New York: Alfred A. Knopf, 1949.

Laqueur, Walter, ed. *A Dictionary of Politics.* New York: Free Press, 1971.

Luttwak, Edward. *A Dictionary of Modern War.* New York: Harper & Row, 1971.

Matthews, Mitford M., ed. *A Dictionary of Americans on Historical Principles.* Chicago: University of Chicago Press, 1951.

New Columbia Encyclopedia, The. 4th ed. Exec. editor, William H. Harris; Manag. editor, Judith Levey. New York: Columbia Univ. Press, forthcoming 1975.

Oxford English Dictionary. Edited by James A. H. Murray, Henry Bradley, W. A. Craigie, and C. T. Onions. Oxford: Clarendon Press, 1933. 13 vols. A corrected reissue, with an introduction, supplement and bibliography of *A New English Dictionary on Historical Principles.*
_____. *Supplement.* vol. 1, A-G. Oxford: Clarendon Press, 1972. Vols. 2 (H-P) and 3 (Q-Z) to be published in intervals of not more than three years.

Plano, Jack C., and Greenberg, Milton. *The American Political Dictionary.* 3d ed. Hinsdale, Ill.: Dryden Press, 1972.

Roberts, Geoffrey K. *A Dictionary of Political Analysis.* New York: St. Martin's Press, 1971.

Safire, William. *The New Language of Politics: A Dictionary of Catchwords, Slogans & Political Usage.* New York: Collier Books, 1972.

Schattschneider, E. E. *Two Hundred Million Americans in Search of a Government.* New York: Holt, Rinehart and Winston, 1969.

Skidmore, Max J., ed. *Word Politics: Essays on Language and Politics.* Palo Alto: James E. Freel & Associates, 1972.

Smith, Edward C., and Zurcher, Arnold J. *Dictionary of American Politics.* 2d ed. New York: Barnes & Noble, 1968.

Webster's New Collegiate Dictionary. 8th in series. Springfield, Mass.: G. & C. Merriam Company, 1973.

Webster's Third New International Dictionary. Edited by Philip Babcock Gove and the Merriam-Webster editorial staff. Springfield, Mass.: G. & C. Merriam Co., 1969.

9. Encyclopedias

Numerous new, specialized encyclopedias published within the past ten years are not only good for openers, are great time-savers and quick reference providers but contain many of the finest articles on social science subjects to be found anywhere. Qualified scholars have often hammered out some of their best work on the anvil of an encyclopedia's requirements to make a clear and authoritative statement about a topic within their special interest. The title of an encyclopedia should not stop one from peering inside—pity the poor editor; it can't be snappy and must be brief. Most titles suggest a domain, but even when it's general and covers the whole world it really has a parochial title *(Americana, Britannica)*, while those that indicate an outlook are often broad in compass even while holding to a point of view *(Catholic, Judaica)*, or representing academic disciples or methodologies *(Education, Philosophy, the Social Sciences)*. Many encyclopedias are too skimpy to claim the name, moreover, while such works as the *Handbook of Social Psychology* and the *Handbook of Political Science* are decidedly encyclopedic in concept, scope and bulk. All of these, and others, should be known as friends to the busy student of political science, and, if used, they deserve ready and unblushing citation.

Because the encyclopedias have one window on the world and I have another, my effort is to focus on entries that fit the most conventional interests of political scientists. Readers should not be deterred from this; it is simply impossible to say in a paragraph what a given encyclopedia covers and what it omits. The aim is simply to call these great sources to the attention of researchers who may have failed to know of them or, knowing, neglected to press them into use.

Chronology is taken as basic in this essay on encyclopedias because time, above all, marks them and sets them apart from each other. Mostly, encyclopedias are superseded, not revised. Thus the *Encyclopaedia of the Social Sciences* of the early 1930s is a landmark and an inspiration but it was published once and only once, albeit reprinted at various points in different bindings. In the late 1960s an *entirely* new work was conceived, written, and executed under the title of the *International Encyclopedia of the Social Sciences*. Both will be discussed here. It should be noted that neither could deal with events yet to unfold, nor could either treat methodologies or portray concepts not yet in circulation. Both certainly are milestones in intellectual history but there they stand, frozen in time. Many of the other encyclopedias also supersede earlier efforts along the same line and, for the most part, they bear self-consciousness by describing their lineages in introductions to the encyclopedias now in vogue that are reviewed in these pages.

Some of the general encyclopedias have striven to keep themselves up to date by issuing yearbooks. These may vary in quality, but an encyclopedia plus thirty yearbooks after it tends to be a most depressing sight. Probably the best thing is to let time pass sufficiently so that a new generation of scholars is aroused enough to attempt an altogether new encyclopedia that grows out of a fresh passion for organizing and presenting the accumulated knowledge. Otherwise there remains the whole library and the *card catalog*– the greatest bibliographical tool prior to the computer finding aids–to aid the student who finds that the encyclopedia he is using is ignorant of the New Deal, or World War II, or the development of game theory, or the newest studies in budgetary theory and practice.

We now proceed to consider, in the order of their publication, several encyclopedias–in name or in function–likely to be of some value to political scientists. (Full citations will be found in the bibliography.)

The *Encyclopaedia of the Social Sciences* was conceived in 1923, organized and executed during the next several years, had the first volume published in 1930, and the final, 15th volume published in 1935. The first volume begins with a series of articles, modern classics, on the development of social thought and institutions by such scholars as Edwin R. A. Seligman, F. J. C. Hearnshaw, Harold J. Laski, Crane Brinton, Charles A. Beard and R. M. MacIver. Among several articles which follow on the social sciences as disciplines is an extended historical account about developments in the United States by L. L. Bernard (1:324-349) which supplies an extended bibliography. The quality of the essays reflects the traits of the disciplines during the period when they were composed, 1925-1935. The political science entries, accordingly, tend to a certain flat formalism well-informed by history and current trends as seen, for example, in Leonard D. White's "Public Administration" (1:440-450), Lindsay Rogers' "Politics" (12:224-226), and the exceptionally interesting essays by Arthur N. Holcombe, Harold F. Gosnell, Arthur MacMahon and others on "Political Parties" (11:589-639). The article by William B.

Munro on "Municipal Government" (11:105-117) exhibits both the values and drawbacks of the straight description with a touch of reform but little analysis that characterized political science in that day. Perhaps the most durable essays in the *Encyclopaedia of the Social Sciences* are those on law, written as they were by the talented group associated with the school of thought known as "legal realism" in its heyday around 1930. Many wrote more than one article of which these are representative: William O. Douglas on "Bankruptcy" (2:449-454); Felix Frankfurter on "Advisory Opinions" (1:475-478), the "Labor Injunction" (8:653-657), and the "Supreme Court of the United States" (14:474-482); Edwin M. Borchard on "Declaratory Judgment" (5:51-52); Thurman Arnold on "Law Enforcement" (9:267-269); Walton H. Hamilton on "Caveat Emptor" (3:280-282), "Constitutionalism" (4:255-258), "Freedom of Contract" (8:450-4550, and especially "Judicial Process" (8:450-456); Walter Wheeler Cook on "Equity" (5:582-588); Jerome Frank on "Lawlessness" (5:277-279); Karl Llewellyn on "Case Law" (3:249-251) and "Case Method" (3:251-254); and Roscoe Pound on "Common Law" (4:50-56), "Jurisprudence" (8:477-492), and the "Rule of Law" (13:463-466). Edward S. Corwin stood somewhat apart from this group but his "Judicial Review" (8:457-463) is fine craftsmanship. Many of these articles stand both as monuments to the dominance of legal realism at the time and remain outstanding expositions worth consultation today. The scholarly apparatus within this encyclopedia are outstanding in their conception around themes located in the exhaustive index in the last volume, in the careful attention to bibliography in all entries, and to the attention given to international themes of emerging importance such as communism, fascism and Zionism. We will see later how the qualities of later social science is reflected in similar encyclopedias in the 1960s.

The *New Catholic Encyclopedia,* 1967, in 15 volumes, lives up to its self-description as "An International Work of Reference on the Teachings, History, Organization, and Activities of the Catholic Church, and on All Institutions, Religions, Philosophies, and Scientific and Cultural Developments Affecting the Catholic Church from Its Beginning to the Present." Prepared at The Catholic University of America in Washington, it has a decidedly world outlook and yet gives heavy attention to intellectual and political matters of special interest in the United States. The range is surprising as there is not only a set of careful articles on "Abortion" (1:27-31) but one on "Abnormal Psychology" (1:24-26), and even "Henry Adams" (1:119-120). There are absolutely impeccable treatments at various points, for which consult the index in volume 15, on Education in the United States, Free-masonry and Anti-Clericalism. There are biographical sketches of numerous Americans who have played roles both large and small in domestic politics: Cardinal Gibbons, Cardinal Spellman, Al Smith, John F. Kennedy and John A. Ryan. The important lobbying group, the National Catholic Welfare Conference, and other organizations are here. A surprising entry, of interest to many political scientists, is the essay on each state in the U.S.A. showing a breakdown of religious groups thereby providing a history of church-state relations nationwide. This is in itself a virtual encyclopedia of the status of the Catholic Church in every state in the Union. I have read several and commend especially the essays on Louisiana and the State of Maine although there is in each case more emphasis on demography, formal history, and statutory and case law than on the political consequences of different religious mixes in the several states.

The Encyclopedia of Philosophy, 8 volumes, 1967, begins with an introduction explaining that the aim of the 1,500 articles is that they be "sufficiently explicit to be read with pleasure and profit by the intelligent nonspecialist" while remaining valuable to the specialist. Political scientists will find the detailed 60 page index in volume 8 intelligently arranged for quick checking. Large subjects such as political philosophy include sub-topics as well as a list of individual philosophers with biographical entries. All the giants—Aristotle, Plato, St. Augustine, Machiavelli, Hobbes, Hume, Locke, Bentham, Mill—and many lesser known figures are here. The essays themselves stress philosophy first, last and always but their politics are also amply explained and criticized. There are numerous typical articles within the domain of political and social theory running alphabetically from the beginning, from anarchism, authority, communism, conservatism, economics and national choice, equality and fascism, to the end with sociology of law, sovereignty, state, toleration, tradition, and utopias and utopianism. There is an article on American philosophy and related ones on ethics, idealism, liberalism, logical positivism and philosophy of law. I count 66 articles on American philosophers—a solid set of biographical and, of course, "philosophical" portraits of famous men, among them Morris Cohen, John Dewey, T. S. Eliot, Thomas Jefferson, Reinhold Neibuhr, William Graham Sumner, Henry David Thoreau, Thorstein Veblen and Alfred North Whitehead.

The *International Encyclopedia of the Social Sciences,* 1968, consists of 17 volumes with the majority of the topical articles being devoted to the concepts, theories, and methods of the ten disciplines of anthropology, economics, geography, history, law, political science, psychiatry, psychology, sociology and statistics. (1:xxii) It also "includes biographies of some six hundred persons whose research and writings have had an impact upon the social sciences." (1:xxiv) Among political writers whose work touched the United States, whose intellectual biographies appear here and are not readily or adequately standard biographical sources are Arthur F. Bentley, Arnold Brecht, James Bryce, Francis W. Coker, Frantz Fanon, Frank J. Goodnow, V. O. Key, Jr., Harold J. Laski, Walter Lippman, A. Lawrence Lowell, Charles H. McIllwain, James Madison, Charles E. Merriam, Robert Michels, Moisei Ia. Ostrogorski and Stuart Rice, Alexis deTocqueville, Westel Woodbury Willoughby and Woodrow Wilson. The *International Encyclopedia of the Social Sciences* is more valuable to political scientists today than any of the other encyclopedias reviewed here. In the index, readers will find hundreds of articles listed under international relations (16:92-93), law (16:93-94), political science (16:96-99), and statistics (16:107-108). To pick and choose articles, and rate them, in such a basic source to the discipline of political science is beyond both my capacity and nerve. An extended critical essay from a political science viewpoint awaits its author. What can be said briefly is that for different research tasks quite different sets of articles will display rewarding relationships. In a study of American state mandatory sexual sterilization laws, for example, consider the general survey of "Eugenics" by Gordon Allen (5:193-197) and the closely related biography of "Francis Galton" by F. N. David (6:48-53). To place the eugenics enthusiasm in the early 20th century into a larger framework than that of pressure group activity, the articles that are pertinent include these: "Intellectuals" by Edward Shils (7:399-415); the two articles on "Social Movements" by Rudolf Heberle (14:438-444) and Joseph R. Gusfield (14:445-452); and finally, "Voluntary Associations: Sociological Aspects" by David L. Sills (16:362-379).

The Encyclopedia of Education's 10 volumes, published in 1971, in more than 1,000 articles "offers a view of the institutions and people, of the processes and products, found in educational practice" as they deal with "history, theory, research and philosophy, as well as the structure and fabric of education." The index, filling all of volume 10, includes a detailed "Directory of Contributors" (10:1-115), a unique reference tool; a large "Guide to Articles" (10:117-228); and an ample, detailed "Index" (10:229-627). Political science students will find many articles of interest, among them these: "History of Universities in the United States," by Robert L. Church (9:341-354); "Urban Education: School Segregation, Desegretation and Integration," by Irwin Katz (9:369-376); "Appropriations Process in Federal Education," by Daniel J. Flood (1:239-245); and "Educational Policy," by James E. McClellan (7:168-181). There are a modest number of thorough biographies, a large number of brief articles about particular organizations such as "Resources for the Future" by Henry Jarrett (7:547-549), and country-by-country assessments of education. There are no articles on particular states or cities.

The *Encyclopaedia Judaica,* first published in the Hebrew language, and in a beautiful English edition in 1972 in 16 volumes, is remarkable for its thoroughness in the pursuit of matters Jewish in all realms of history, of thought, in geography and, of course, in politics. Thus the entries for countries (Spain, Sweden, the United States—all one would expect and then some) are about Jews and Jewish relations in those countries. This is true as well for countless cities from obvious ones such as Smolensk, Vienna and New York to Washington, D.C. and Portland, Oregon. The most fascinating and poignant articles for me include "Vital Statistics" (16:178-190), "Anti-Semitic Political Parties and Organizations" (3:79-87), "Anti-Semitism" (3:87-159), and the most overwhelming of all, "Holocaust" (8:828-906). Compared to these, articles on Jewish sportsmen and biographies of minor figures help bring life back to an agreeable human scale. There are numerous biographical sketches, a short but incisive one on the political writings of Hannah Arendt, not surprisingly critical, and a laudatory essay on Louis D. Brandeis. There is a short, really inadequate treatment of the Rosenberg case. There is much about Israel, of course, of its founders like David Ben Gurion and its wars, including the Sinai Campaign of 1956 and the Six Day War of 1967. Maps, posters, cartoons, photographs and charts are profuse and add much enlightenment. The article on "Advertising" (2:317-319) even includes a witty and winning ad from the series "You don't have to be Jewish to Love Levy's real Jewish rye." Beginning articles on several organizations or movements of special interest to students of American politics are these: "American Jewish Archives" (2:822), "American Jewish Committee" (2:822-825), "American Jewish Congress" (2:825-826), "B'nai B'rith" (4:1143-1149), and "Zionism" (16:1031-1162).

The *Dictionary of the History of Ideas,* 4 volumes, 1973, includes 313 essays on the physical and biological sciences, anthropology, psychology, religion, philosophy, literature, linguistics and formal mathematical ideas. Most political scientists will dwell on the 59 articles dealing with "the historical development of economic, legal, and political ideas and institutions, ideologies, and movements." (Preface, 1:viii). There is no index so that connections in this somewhat idiosyncratic reference book are often difficult to follow. Yet its relatively small compass allows one simply to turn the pages to discover gems, among them these articles by political scientists: "Academic Freedom" and "Constitutionalism" by David Fellman, "Socialism from Antiquity to Marx" by Sanford Lakoff, "Despotism" by Melvin Richter, and "General Will" by Judith N. Shklar. I did not generally find the articles on law satisfactory largely because they did not feed my provincial interest in American law. Stephen R. Graubard's essay on "Democracy" explicates the history of the subject and concludes with adequate representations of the views of Schumpeter, Dahl and Lipset. That this is a formidable and worthwhile collection is attested to by numerous other articles such as those of Kenneth Arrow's "Formal Theories of Social Welfare," Moshe Barasch's "The City," Hans Kohn's "Nationalism," Edward H. Madden's "Civil Disobedience," and Oskar Morgenstern's "Game Theory."

Preparation of the 15th edition of *The New Encyclopaedia Britannica* in 30 volumes, published in 1974, took 27 years and, according to the *Wall Street Journal*, cost $32 million, not including printing. (Edmund Fuller, "Summing It All Up in 43 Million Words," *Wall Street Journal*, May 28, 1974, p. 20.) This is brought to us by the man who taught us *How to Read a Book*, and gave us the *Syntopicon* to *The Great Ideas (The Great Ideas: A Syntopicon of Great Books of the Western World)*. Mortimer J. Adler is General Editor of the *New Britannica*, and is dedicated to the notion that all knowledge is organized hierarchically (though this is disguised as a circle), and displays discomfort with the way life is lived today. Libraries wishing to serve political science may do better to invest in specialized encyclopedias and in other reference books than to spend $598 for this ill-arranged, cumbersome, often outdated set that is destined to age fast.

Readers of articles about politics like to know, and need to know, authors' names yet these are disguised at the end of articles with initials that can be guessed at or deciphered by going back to the first of these 30 volumes. There one finds a listing alphabetically by, of all things, the beginning initials of the author so that A. Zy. (Antoni Zygmund) comes before Z. I. A. (Zafar I. Ansari). Of the seven other references discussed in this chapter on encyclopedias only the *Judaica* uses the same system. Numerous articles do not indicate an author at all and there is frequent indication that the editors aided an author substantially by reworking or completing an article.

Many of the political science authors were already prominent a generation ago and their articles exhibit viewpoints then in vogue. The article on "Special Interest Groups" (Macropaedia 17: 445-449) by S. E. F. (Samuel E. Finer), the able British political scientist, argues that interest groups in Sweden and America are similar, but both text and bibliography lack reference to the work of David Truman, Bauer, Dexter and Pool or to any of the numerous detailed studies of the place of interest groups in litigation in the United States. Nor do these matters appear to be picked up elsewhere.

Some of the encyclopedists, and I intend the double entendre, have been given more space in this 15th edition over what they had for their articles in the 14th edition and they have put it to good use. Thus, does D. Fe. (David Fellman) provide a thorough discourse on "Constitutional Law" (Macropaedia 5:85-93) with dependable distinctions between unitary and federal systems on the one hand and those between presidential and parliamentary systems on the other. His discussion of the unique role of the Supreme Court of the United States through its power of judicial review is as good as they come. So, too, does Ea. L. (Earl Latham) prove his mettle in broadening and updating his essay on "Political Science" (Macropaedia 14:702-714). His learned history of how the discipline came into being is capped by a winning assessment of the behavioral persuasion in political science as, perhaps, not much more than what happened after World War II. Not that this is flip; the essay develops the subject quite fully.

Although cross-references occasionally appear within the long articles in the Macropaedia, they are absent following them. They are very greatly missed even though Adler and the many admiring reviewers of *The New Encyclopaedia Britannica* believe this lack is compensated by the one volume Propaedia, not "an" but *the* "Outline of Knowledge and Guide to the Britannica." Readers are urged to use this volume "when the knowledge you are seeking is at a high level of generality, or when you intend to pursue a systematic course of reading or study in the Britannica." Thus would a political science student turn there to the fifth of ten subjects, titled "Human Society," first reading the essay on "Man the Social Animal" (Propaedia: 280-282) by Harold Lasswell. This part is then broken down into divisions, as follows: I. Culture. II. Social organization and social change. III. The production, distribution, and utilization of wealth. IV. Politics and government. V. Law. VI. Education. As in all the other parts and sections to which that on "politics and government" are similar there is a listing of articles in the arabic-numbered 19-volume Macropaedia, none with an indication of the authors or of possible cross references. In a sense the Micropaedia of 10 volumes using Roman numerals is the index to the entire set. This part of the encyclopaedia is chock full of entries which include abstracts of the substantial essays to be found in the Macropaedia, concise entries of 100,000 matters all told and numerous charts, photographs and other illustrations. Here there are cross references. The fact that I did not find many words such as adjudication, ghetto and litigation may only mean that the Micropaedia is no substitute for a dictionary. But for 30 volumes that cost so much to produce as well as to purchase, the lack of consistent cross references and a true index is a substantial inconvenience.

Again comparing the *Britannica* to the other sources examined in this chapter, all but the small *Dictionary of the History of Ideas* have full indexes and it, like nearly all the other six encyclopedias have analytical tables of contents.

This inconvenience along with the curious way in which the reader must go to great pains to identify authors are among the crotchets that Mortimer Adler is famous for. There is no other way to account for his insistence on the diphthong "ae" and its closure in the printer's ligature in Propaedia (one volume), Micropaedia (10 volumes), and Macropaedia (19 volumes). Again, only the *Encyclopaedia of The Social Sciences* of 40 years ago and the *Encyclopaedia Juadica,* published in Jerusalem, not in Chicago, use this spelling. How the Rube Goldberg of knowledge will keep this up-to-date is a question mark although "the salesman who called" told me he expected annual supplements.

The conscious plan of the 15th edition of the *Britannica* to afford a world view, throughout the history, of the subjects chosen for delineation badly serves political science in general, and American political studies in particular. In the article "Political Parties" (Macropaedia 14:677-684) neither the text nor bibliography by M. Du./Ed. (Maurice Duverger and the editors) even allude to the publications of Pendleton Herring, V. O. Key, E. E. Schattschneider, or Leon D. Epstein. In the article "Political Philosophy" (Macropaedia 14:684-697) by J. E. B. (John E. Bowle) lays theory stress on the history of political philosophy and, in our times, on Marxism and irrationalism. The article gives some attention to deTocqueville, Lewis Mumford, James Burnham and, especially, Herbert Marcuse. There is not a word of Madison or Calhoun, let alone of David Riesman, Robert Dahl, Seymour Martin Lipset, or Sheldon Wolin. The article on "Budgets, Governmental" (Macropaedia 3:441-445) by unnamed hands has worthy treatments of the theory of public goods, program budgeting and cost-benefit analysis but it merely cites Wildavsky's 1964 book, *The Politics of the Budgetary Process,* rather than present its theme. Articles are mentioned only in some bibliographies, none in this one, so that the early work of V. O. Key and the more recent studies of Wildavsky go unmentioned. Yet "Electoral Process" (Macropaedia 6:527-535) by H. E./R. G. (Heinz Eulau and Roger Gibbons) manages to pull a strong thread of analysis and reach sound generalizations on such topics as elections in authoritarian systems, proportional methods of voting, plebiscites, apportionment and the social sources of nonvoting. At least its bibliography includes Angus Campbell *et al*, *The American Voter* (1960), the only mention in this *Britannica*, so far as I can see, of survey research in the United States. It seemed possible that these slights to American political scientists might be repaired in the Micropaedia but a close check reveals only two entries of note. Charles Merriam is omitted but his student Harold Lasswell is nicely sketched with many of his publications included and with cross-references at the end to communication, propaganda and the psychological approach to politics. (Micropaedia VI: 62.) The latter reference is to Latham's discussion of Merriam, Lasswell and Gosnell in the article, already mentioned here, on "Political Science." There is also a short, inept, who's who type biography of V. O. Key (Micropaedia V: 777-778) without cross references.

It may be that encyclopedias are by their nature helpful tools within a library where the card catalog and other sources are available. The year 1975 is expected to bring a new specialized *Handbook of Political Science* in 8 volumes. This will be a welcome addition, functionally speaking, to the specialized encyclopedia field.

Also in 1975 the one-volume *New Columbia Encyclopedia's* 4th edition will again offer the most concise treatment of geographical, biographical and historical and other information to be found easily in between two covers. Read about "hell" and then follow the cross references to "heaven" and "sin" for a start on Christian theology. On people it is the best place to sort out the Presidents Adams, Senators Kennedy and Congressmen Fish. There are histories of copyright and of trade unions, excellent essays on wars and particular military engagements. If one looks up Danbury Hatters' Case the cross-reference is to "injunction" which, in turn, will lead to a quick review of the history of the common law and of the American labor movement. All the editions are good: the 1st in 1935, the 2nd in 1950, the 3rd in 1963 and, hopefully and expectantly, the 4th in 1975.

Bibliography

Dictionary of the History of Ideas. Editor in chief, Philip P. Wiener. 4 vols. New York: Charles Scribner's Sons, 1973.

Encyclopedia Americana. 30 vols. New York, Chicago: Encyclopedia Americana. 1st ed. 1903-04, 16 vols.

Encyclopaedia Judaica. 16 vols. New York: Macmillan; Jerusalem, Israel: Encyclopaedia Judaica Jerusalem, 1972.

Encyclopedia of Education. Editor in chief, Lee C. Deighton. 10 vols. New York: Macmillan and the Free Press, 1971.

Encyclopedia of Philosophy. Editor in chief, Paul Edwards. 8 vols. New York: Macmillan, 1967.

Encyclopaedia of the Social Sciences. Editor in chief, E. R. A. Seligman; assoc. editor, Alvin Johnson. 15 vols. New York: Macmillan, 1930-1935.

Handbook of Political Science, The. Edited by Fred I. Greenstein and Nelson W. Polsby. 8 vols. Reading, Mass.: Addison-Wesley Pub. Co., forthcoming 1975.

Handbook of Social Psychology, The. Edited by Gardner Lindzey and Elliot Aronson. 6 vols. 2d ed. Reading, Mass.: Addison-Wesley Pub. Co., 1968-1970.

International Encyclopedia of the Social Sciences. Edited by David L. Sills. 17 vols. New York: Macmillan and the Free Press, 1968.

New Catholic Encyclopedia. Editor in chief, William J. McDonald. 15 vols. New York: McGraw-Hill Book Co., 1967.

New Columbia Encyclopedia, The. 4th ed. Exec. editor, William H. Harris; Manag. editor, Judith Levey. New York: Columbia Univ. Press, forthcoming 1975.

New Encyclopaedia Britannica, The. 30 vols. Gen. editor, Mortimer J. Adler. Chicago: Encyclopaedia Britannica, 1974. 1st ed., 1768-71, 3 vols.

Part Three: The Political Scientist in the Library

10. Library Basics

Viewing the quantity of books available in the library, one could mistakenly conclude that libraries are simply collections of books. To do so would be a hasty underestimation of the potential of the library as a research source. Libraries, in addition to their more prominently displayed books, include all other forms of information in which man's knowledge is recorded. Periodicals, manuscripts, films, recordings, and microfilms and microfiche can all be found in libraries. The use of these resources by researchers generally provides a much more comprehensive view of a subject than would be available through "book research" alone.

The *American Library Directory* is a classified state-by-state list of libraries in the United States and Canada which provides personnel and statistical data. The *1974-1975 Directory* lists 28,036 libraries in those two countries. Public libraries and their branches, college and university libraries, special libraries, and law, medical, and religious libraries are included.

In the *Directory* libraries are listed geographically by state and city, and under town or city alphabetically by name. For each library the following information is provided:

1) Name, address and telephone number
2) Personnel
3) Number of volumes
4) Microform holdings
5) Income and expenditures
6) Information on microfilming and reading facilities, audiovisual materials, and document depositories (mainly U.S. Government, also state, United Nations, and other agencies)
7) Subject interests and special collections

One can also find, for public libraries, information on circulation, branch libraries, bookmobiles, and data on membership in regional systems. For college and university libraries, special information provided includes (1) the most recent enrollment figures, (2) the year in which the library was established, and (3) lists of department, school, or branch libraries forming part of university and college library systems.

The arrangement of information about libraries affords a rough sociological glimpse of various communities. But almost anyone who is not a professional will learn an astonishing amount about available resources in a given locality. Thus a state capital like Augusta, Maine has related state libraries while the small city of Bangor has a public library with perhaps more volumes and a higher rate of circulation per capita of any community in the country. The library resources of Amherst, Massachusetts are remarkable, yet characteristic of numerous college towns elsewhere.

As reference materials, newspapers, magazines and journals constitute major resources for the social scientist and particularly for the student of politics. Equally important to the serious researcher is the material that is now available to facilitate the use of these resources. Newspapers, magazines and journals are important sources in and of themselves, but when our usage is aided by the indexes, guides and abstracts available in libraries, the wealth of the material contained in these sources is given substantially more utility.

The daily newspaper is perhaps the most readily available of all. The initial chronicler of the events of the day after radio and television, the newspaper is read for what it says and studied for how it says it. As a record of unfolding events, however, the newspaper is not without its defects and a word of caution is in order. The reliability (and thus the objectivity) of a newspaper is the most frequent target of contemporary criticism. It is a good idea to keep in mind that while newspapers like to think they print all the "news" objectively they merely abstract a few events out of the current scene, and stories describe these happenings. The decision as to which events to abstract is how newspapers differentiate themselves, one from the other.

The *Middletown* (Connecticut) *Press* or the *Fort Collins Coloradan* are not expected to print a complete account of the day's events; indeed, few people expect these and similar newspapers to be either complete or accurate in their record of daily events. "Newspapers of record," however, like the *Times* of London and the *New York Times* have taken on a special obligation to print "all the news." To the extent that they do not, they can be justly criticized. In recent years the *New York Times* has become the target of criticism by those who believe it has failed, at least in part, in its self-defined task. The late-lamented Nixon Administration has charged that the American mass media, especially television network news programs, the *New York Times* and the *Washington Post* are biased in their selection and presentation of "the news." They did not adduce evidence to prove it, however.

A library's card catalog is a giant reference tool. The drawers and drawers of cards here are in Olin Library, Wesleyan University, Middletown, CT. This fabulous tool is being replaced at the New York Public Library by a speedier dictionary catalog looking much like a telephone book. (*New York Times,* Nov. 29, 1972, p. 47.) This approach may spread.

In spite of the criticism leveled at these publications, the "newspaper of record" is a valuable resource for the political scientist studying the recent or distant past. The newspaper often provides the *only* resource material available on a contemporary event that is not yet covered in popular magazines or scholarly journals.

The *Index to the Times* (London) and the *New York Times Index* are quality reference materials on par in importance with the material they index. These indexes are the exclusive key to the relevant reference material in the respective newspaper file and the skeletal key to the chronology of unfolding events. They are perhaps the contemporary reference books most needed and most heavily used by students of social, economic, and political developments. Typically, though, newspapers and their indexes have rarely been scrutinized by social scientists for accuracy, completeness and quality of interpretation. Still, the newspapers of record with indexes remain important combinations of reference materials and reference books, and the *New York Times Index* deserves extended attention here.

The *New York Times* is a record in print of the world's events which covers major global and national events (as well as a lot of other, not-so-major events.) The *New York Times Index (NYTI)* classifies, twice a month, this news alphabetically by subject, person, organization and geographical locations thus providing an easy-to-use, comprehensive and generally (since it is found in most college and university libraries) easily obtainable record of important day-to-day events. Information relating to

business and financial affairs, political developments, governmental activities and actions, and international affairs is easily located in the *Index*. Furthermore, the *Index* can be used to
- check names of places and dates of events
- verify names, initials and titles of public officials and other persons in the news
- locate texts of bills, resolutions, speeches, international agreements and court decisions
- locate the full text of an article, review, biography, obituary, etc., in the body of the *Times*
- track down stories in any newspaper or news periodical.

In addition, the summary in the *NYTI* may contain the essential facts needed, often making further searching unnecessary.

Other newspapers with their own indexes of interest to the political scientist include the *Wall Street Journal* with its *Wall Street Journal Index*, the *Christian Science Monitor* and the *Subject Index of the Christian Science Monitor*, and the *National Observer* and the *National Observer Index*. These publications differ widely in scope from the *New York Times*, and they make no effort to provide the record of events that it does. They are, however, quite useful after a topic has been defined or when an issue is being researched for leads to investigative reports, substantive articles and editorial analysis.

It must be noted that although few newspapers can claim to be newspapers of record, in many instances the local newspaper will be the best (and often the only) source of information about locally important historical or contemporary political affairs, controversies, or prominent people. For example, the political science student researching the 1930-1935 politics of flood control along the Connecticut River would not fare well by consulting the *New York Times*. A wiser and much more fruitful approach would be to consult the local newspapers of the towns which abut the river in Connecticut, Massachusetts, Vermont and New Hampshire. Middletown, thus having been found as a likely town, search for information about its local publications would then be in order. Since the flood is an historical event, the best prospect would be to check *American Newspapers, 1821-1936: A Union List of Files Available in the United States and Canada* (better known as the *Union List of Newspapers*). This *Union List of Newspapers* contains a geographical listing by state of newspapers published during those years, and it indicates at what libraries one can find particular newspapers. Among the several entries for Middletown, the best bet would be the *Middletown Press* since other listings ceased publications prior to 1931.

Had the event being researched been of a more recent vintage, reference would more properly have been to the Library of Congress's *Newspapers in Microform: United States, 1948-1972* for Middletown. This publication lists 34,289 titles in 7,457 localities, and as libraries put their bulky newspaper holdings on the more economical and durable microforms available, these numbers will surely increase.

Students of politics should realize that two gaps exist in the bibliographic listing of newspapers. First there is no up-to-date list of newspapers published from 1936 to 1948; thus there is no definite way to check publications issued during these years and their locations. Second, and probably of more importance, there is not a *Union List of Newspapers* after 1936. Although some access is provided to the post 1936 years by the Library of Congress publication, *Newspapers in Microform* lists only those papers stored on microfilm. Missing are the cumulations of local newspapers in local libraries, historical societies, and even large university libraries where the cost of putting on microfilm extensive newspaper holdings has been deemed, at least in part, too expensive. The diligent researcher will have to check thoroughly probable holders of local newspapers (especially local historical societies, local libraries, and, if the publication is still in existence, the newspaper's own "library" or "morgue") in the hope of coming across an elusive local source.

The Photoduplication Service of the Library of Congress accepts as the definition of a newspaper: "Any periodical publication, put on sale to the general public, which serves as the initial source of written news of current events." (*Newspapers in Microform: United States* p. viii, preface.) *Facts on File* and *Keesing's Contemporary Archives* are two mass media print publications which, although they are neither sold to the general public nor the initial source of the written news and thus cannot properly be called newspapers, can be quite useful to the political scientist as tools similar in substance and scope to the newspaper of record.

Facts on File, "the weekly national and foreign news reference service with cumulative index," is a publication which provides easy access to past and present events. Established in 1940 it provides a comprehensive weekly digest of national and foreign news with a twice monthly, cumulative index. One advantage of the digest is the more balanced coverage provided. Primary sources used by *Facts on File* to gather, integrate, cross-check, and balance the information it presents are the *New York Times,* the *Washington Post,* the *Wall Street Journal, Miami Herald,* Toronto *Globe and Mail, Times* of London, *Le Monde* of Paris, and *La Prensa* of Buenos Aires. Periodical sources used include American news magazines, the British *Economist,* Mexico's *Vision, Africa Recorder, Africa Report, Asian Recorder,* and the *Far East Economic Review* (Hong Kong). Other supplementary sources of information include the British Broadcasting Corporation's Monitoring Service (which covers domestic news broadcasts from countries in Africa, Asia, the Middle East, and the Soviet Block); Moscow's Novosti News Agency (which covers the primary newspapers of the U.S.S.R.); and the U.S. Government's Foreign Broadcast Information Service (which reports on selected foreign radio station transmissions). Finally, publications such as the *Congressional Record,* the *State Department Bulletin, Weekly Compilation of Presidential Documents,* and the press releases of federal agencies, foreign governments, the United Nations, and voluntary associations are used to complete the factual picture.

The Index to *Facts on File* is both a tool and a source. It identifies, dates and locates every item of factual information in the weekly digest making it possible to track down and verify facts.

A similar loose-leaf reference tool published in London since 1931 is *Keesing's Contemporary Archives* which digests the important events throughout the world in weekly "News Sheets." Its biweekly index provides instant access to the accumulating news sheets. *Keesing's* provides details and data as well as much *more* extensive documentation than found in *Facts on File.* Its coverage of international affairs is exhaustive, and background information provided in the text to supply the reader with a sufficient basis for understanding the event being studied is complete and quite useful. *Keesing's* is not a substitute for *Facts on File;* indeed, they differ radically in scope, content, and style. The two taken together, however, provide a handy beginning or quick double-check for research on global and national affairs. *Keesing's* is exceptionally good reading.

Facts on File, Inc. also publishes *Editorials on File,* a "twice-monthly newspaper editorial survey with cumulative index." *Editorials on File* is a reference service which provides a survey of the editorial content in 151 newspapers (August, 1974) across the United States and Canada and a monthly subject index cumulated quarterly. The Editorial Surveys are introduced by a brief summary of the events that stimulated the editorials.

After an event's appearance in and coverage by the mass media press, the reporting and interpretation of the event passes from the newspaper and the news digest services to the weekly and monthly magazines and quarterly journals. Unfortunately, there is no master index to this vast amount of periodical literature in, and of relevance to, social science; and periodical sources can only be tapped through a complex set of indexes. The most valuable type of index is usually one for a single publication or journal, provided one's interest in and use of that particular periodical is high. In partial solution to the compound problem of having no general index and only too specialized indexes for particular journals, most disciplines, political science among them, have developed separate indexes and abstracts through their respective national and international associations.

From 1906 to December, 1966, each issue of the *American Political Science Review* contained extensive bibliographic sections on the different fields in political science. This "Selected Articles and Documents" section was a classified listing under various topics (e.g., "Political Theory," "American Government and Politics," "International Law and Relations") of articles in the discipline which had appeared in major English and foreign language journals. The "Selected Articles and Documents" section was a helpful aid for the political scientist trying to keep up with the literature in particular fields; and as a research tool, the section was (and is) a significant help to scholars with a particular topic that needs researching over time.

Oddly enough, however, a complete subject listing of articles within the *A.P.S.R.* itself was not published until 1964, and updated in 1969. Prior to that time, the only tool available for locating material in the *Review* was the annual author-title index in the December issue. Janda's *Cumulative Index to the American Political Science Review, Volumes 1-62: 1906-1968* is a computer produced "keyword-in-context" (KWIC) index to the 2,822 articles appearing in the *A.P.S.R.* during those years. The *Cumulative Index* also includes an alphabetical author's index.

Additional information about articles in the discipline can also be found in the *International Political Science Abstracts*. Published since 1950, in both French and English, the abstracts are confined to articles published in nearly 80 social science journals in some 25 countries. In a handful of journals, all of the articles are abstracted. In most, though, only the articles bearing on political science are selected. This is a solid index, with subject and author listings, and it is an invaluable source of information for a scholar seeking a comprehensive view of writings on a given subject treated by professional students of politics.

The *International Bibliography of Political Science* is one of four parts of the *International Bibliography of the Social Sciences* and is published annually by the International Committee for Social Science Information and Documentation. The *IBPS* is an unannotated index to books, pamphlets, articles, reports, and reviews in over 1,000 major and minor journals of political science. The indexing is selective rather than complete. Entries are multilingual and are classified by a complex "Classification Scheme" which includes broad topics (e.g., Political Though, Governmental Process), sub-classifications (e.g., under Governmental Process: Political influence and trends, General studies, Pressure groups) as well as separate author and subject indexes. This is certainly one of the most comprehensive indexes available, but it may be too complex and cumbersome for a research project with a national (rather than an international or methodological) scope. The two-year publication lag presents further complications.

To "fill the gap created by the discontinuance of the list of articles [the "Selected Articles and Documents" section] in the *American Political Science Review,"* a new service was established in March, 1969, which seeks to "meet the need of political scientists for current bibliographic information in their fields of interest." *ABC Pol Sci: Advance Bibliography of Contents: Political Science and Government* is a reference service which surveys the contents of over 300 periodicals of political science and government. *ABC Pol Sci* reproduces these tables of contents, in advance of or concurrent with the original publication, of these selected "core" journals. Published eight times a year, each issue contains (1) a list of the serial publications covered in that issue, (2) the table of contents of these serials, and (3) subject, law and author indexes. The December issue of each volume is a cumulative annual index; and a cumulative five-year index was published in the spring of 1974.

A publication that appeared about the same time as *ABC Pol Sci* is *Current Contents: Social and Behavioral Sciences* (formerly *CC: Behavioral, Social & Educational Sciences*). Published weekly, *Current Contents* reproduces "in their original format and frequently in advance of publication, the table of contents of more than 1,000 journals reporting world-wide research and practice in the social and behavioral sciences." *Current Contents* limits its coverage of these journals to reproducing the table of contents and an author index and a subject index. Generally the student of political science will find *Current Contents* to be of marginal use: it simply covers too many journals from many other social and behavioral science fields thus making it hard to find particularly relevant articles on a selected topic in political science. Too, it seems to duplicate the coverage of *ABC Pol Sci* which concentrates exclusively on the literature in political science and government.

In addition to the bibliographic sources and table of content reproducing services named above, there are also a handful of keys to periodical sources likely to be of utmost interest to political scientists. For a starter, the *Public Affairs Information Service Bulletin (PAIS)* is excellent. Begun at the New York Public Library in 1914 by a progressive reformer to enable his associates and compatriots to back up their proposals with references, the orientation of *PAIS* is around topics and issues. The *PAIS* is published "weekly except for the last two weeks of each quarter. It is cumulated five times a year, the fifth and final cumulation being a bound volume for permanent reference." *PAIS* is a selective subject index to the literature — books, pamphlets, government documents, periodical articles, organization's reports, etc. — in the field of economics, political science, public affairs and law. Indexers compiling the *PAIS* search widely among hundreds of sources to provide the best resource material on current topics — a must for research in political science.

As periodical indexes go, the *PAIS,* now published by a non-profit association of libraries, is unique. In the periodical index field, the H. W. Wilson Company is preeminent. Its twelve publications strictly limit the number of periodicals indexes — a total of about 1,200. The *Readers' Guide to Periodical Literature* is its best seller, indexing articles from 150 publications of general circulation: *Atlantic, Harper's, Saturday Review, New Republic, Nation, Time, Newsweek,* the *New Yorker,* and the best known and established magazines representing a group outlook: *America* and *Commonweal* for Catholics, the *Christian Century* for liberal Protestants, and *Commentary* for the American Jewish Committee. The list indexed has been changed many times since the *Readers' Guide* took up where *Poole's Index* left off at the turn of the century.

The Wilson Company has been eminently practical in satisfying the needs of libraries. Its prices are scaled to accord with the number of indexed periodicals purchased by specific libraries. In turn, the selection of the magazines indexed is made by these libraries. Some of the details of this practice are an interesting reflection of the particular population of voters. Every seven years lists are prepared by the Committee on Wilson Indexes, which is appointed by the Reference Services Division of the American Library Association. Most of the votes cast are from small public libraries and from many high school and junior college libraries. Large university libraries and large public libraries each have one vote. While it is difficult to believe that this arrangement can ever be altered through litigation to accord with a library's circulation or user figures, it is tempting to recommend changes to accommodate professional readers. This is not to say that the Wilson Company policy is anything but proper within the bounds of its assumptions and its tried-and-true commercial experience. When the voting lists are sent out:

The subscribers are asked by the Committee to cast their votes carefully and objectively, with primary emphasis on the reference value of the periodicals upon which they are voting. They are also urged to give serious consideration to the maintenance of a good subject balance so that no important field will be overlooked in proportion to the overall coverage. Suggestions for additions or deletions of titles should be brought to the attention of the Committee in care of The H. W. Wilson Company.

Most political scientists will find the list of periodicals indexed in the *Social Sciences Index,* as of June 1974, with too many gaps to be a dependable guide to current work in the discipline. Happily, those included are the *Annals of the American Academy of Political and Social Science, American Political Science Review, Canadian Journal of Political Science, Journal of Politics, Orbis, Political Quarterly, Political Science Quarterly, Political Studies, Public Administration Review, Public Opinion Quarterly, Social Research, Soviet Studies, Western Political Quarterly* and *World Politics.* Among the omissions are journals that are included in other Wilson indexes. Their *Readers' Guide to Periodical Indexes,* for example, already carries *Foreign Affairs* and the *Yale Review,* so these are not repeated. Important among the missing in any of these standard indexes are relatively new journals. These include the *British Journal of Political Science,* the *American Journal of Political Science* (formerly the *Midwest Journal of Political Science*), *Polity* and the *Social Science Quarterly* (formerly the *Southwest Journal of Social Sciences*). But its subscribers are not likely to advocate that *every* discipline have anything like full representation for its publications. Precisely 263 periodicals are now covered in the *Social Sciences Index.*

An important rite of passage for a new magazine from an uncertain business venture to an established position is anointment by inclusion in the Wilson indexes. Owing to reliance on infrequent elections, it is a certainty that the first volume of a new periodical would not be included in, say, the *Readers' Guide.* A check of back issues of this index reveals that *Time* magazine, started in 1923, was first included in the *Readers' Guide to Periodical Literature* twelve years later, in 1935. The *New Yorker,* perhaps the foremost political weekly in the broad sense over its first fifty years, was counted in 1930, five years after its first issue. Even *Life,* begun in 1936, and *The Reporter,* begun in 1949, each took four years to make it. Finally, William F. Buckley's conservative *National Review* made it, after a fight, in eight years.

Other standard Wilson indexes deal with agriculture, business, education and technology and will only be of interest to political scientists

There is no such thing as a complete, comprehensive periodical index, but by using all five of the abstracts and indexes above the researcher will locate most of the best known articles on American politics. It is wise to check the temporary updated indexes along with the bound volumes.

with a curiosity in those fields. The *Index to Legal Periodicals* shows further the advantages and limitations inherent in indexing a list of journals. In the *Index to Legal Periodicals* even beginning law reviews are included from their very first volume for the advisory committee speaks for the Association of American Law Schools. But the chief weakness in coverage lies in the omission of all the articles on legislation, litigation, lawyers and law topics in periodicals of general circulation like the *New York Times Magazine,* in the history and in the social science journals. The index is correctly named, in any event, but it is a departure from the *Index to Legal Periodical Literature* by Jones and Chipman for the years 1803 to 1937 for this included a selection of publications in addition to law reviews. It is clear, however, that no one key will do and so the bright researcher must develop peripheral vision in order to notice how helpful at the margins particular indexes may be.

One cannot discuss periodical sources and indexes to these resources without also discussing the procedure by which one can locate holdings of a particular periodical or journal. The researcher will often find that he has the reference to the article he needs, but the modest holdings of the library may not include obscure, or out of print periodicals. The *Union List of Serials in Libraries of the United States and Canada* is the place to begin in order to locate a library which has the periodical being sought This *Union List* is an alphabetical list of over 150,000 serial titles with keys to indicate (1) which university and public libraries have a particular title, (2) what volumes of it they have, and (3) whether photocopies or microfilms can be furnished. *New Serial Titles: A Union List of Serials Commencing Publication After December 31, 1949; 1950-1970 Cumulative* is a twenty-one year compilation which serves "as a continuing supplement to the *Union List of Serials* in the matter of new titles" and carries the same information. *New Serial Titles* appears regularly in eight monthly issues, four quarterly issues and in annual cumulations.

Two commercial publications worth noting are the *Annual Ayer Directory of Publications* and *Ulrich's International Periodical Directory*. *Ayer's* is a directory of the print media—newspapers, magazines and journals—with a geographical catalog of newspapers and periodicals and a classified list with over 900 categories to enable the researcher to find quickly publications of a special or particular interest. *Ulrich's* is a listing of "approximately 55,000 in-print periodicals published throughout the world." *Ulrich's International Periodical Directory* is a subject listing of periodicals which provides plentiful publication information. It also indicates the type of index provided in the publication and the general index in which a particular publication can be located. Unfortunately, this information is not always complete. The *APSR* entry, for example, would indicate that the *APSR* is indexed only in the *International Political Science Abstracts* when, in fact, the *Review* is indexed in the *Social Sciences Index,* the *International Bibliography of Political Science, ABC Pol Sci, Current Contents* and the new *Social Sciences Citation Index.*

Card Catalog Headings

After being chronicled in daily or weekly newspapers, monthly magazines and quarterly journals, books and library shelves come to be the final resting place of the event that was yesterday's "news." Books, of course, are much more than that, and the wealth of material available in print is quite obviously beyond description. Yet to be able to effectively mine these treasures, reference tools are once again needed.

The immediate problem of "subject headings" is unavoidable for anyone at all concerned with political science, government, politics or public affairs. Library users will benefit from an acquaintance with the one volume guide called *Subject Headings Used in the Dictionary Catalogs of the Library of Congress,* which has quarterly supplements. The H. W. Wilson Company periodical indexes follow the dictates of that volume. Library catalogs throughout the United States are also organized upon this book of subject headings. The Card Division of the Library of Congress studies each book processed and indicates the most suitable subject entries for the catalog card prepared for a book. These are listed on the printed card issued by the Library of Congress and several identical cards are purchased by most libraries that acquire a given book. A library's card catalog will include references to a single book many times over. Consider the book entitled *Jumbos and Jackasses: A Popular History of the Political Wars* by Edwin P. Hoyt (Doubleday, 1960). Six cards are needed, one is an author entry and another a title entry. Then there are four subject entries: (1) U.S. Politics and Government; (2) U.S. Presidents. Election; (3) Democratic Party; and (4) Republican Party. The common sense of the Card Division is attested by the fact that the book was *not* cataloged under genus *elephantidae* or genus *equus*.

Microforms

The likelihood of finding pertinent information on microfilm rather than on a printed page is increasing rapidly. Technological reasons, quite apart from the obvious photographic developments, account for this. The change from mostly cotton-fibre paper to mostly wood-pulp paper in the late nineteenth century cut the durability of books, magazines and newspapers fantastically. Newsprint is especially fragile so that libraries have tended to get rid of back volumes of the bound *New York Times* and get the paper on microfilm instead. This, in turn, is a great space saver as two weeks of the *Times* comes on a single microfilm reel, very small, very light. Enterprising companies like University Microfilm-a Xerox Company, Bell & Howell, and the Microfilming Corporation of America have scoured the country to find out-of-print books, little-known magazines, rarities of every kind to film for sale to libraries that are often too new to have colonial documents or books which had limited editions printed. The American Political Science Association, for instance, offers microfilm copies of the mimeographed papers presented by scholars at its annual meetings. It would be just about impossible to think of how one could gain access to papers in this form, every year, by any other means. If items on film are not obtainable in one's own library, microfilm items are usually obtainable through interlibrary loan. Borrowing is often a much better deal for obscure items than purchasing.

The *Microform Review* offers critical comments on microfilm items put out by the government or commercially and affords a good chance for consumers — especially librarians — to decide whether such items as the full filing of the papers of 24 Presidents available from the Library of Congress for $20,000 is worth the price of two Porsches. There are also more modest items available, such as a short reel called the *Kent State University Disorders,* issued by the Micro Photo Division of Bell & Howell, in 1971, for $15.00. By looking closely at this item we can see in fuller detail the advantages and disadvantages of microfilm sources.

The *Akron Beacon Journal,* like all newspapers as we understand them, has a morgue, a clip-file of back issues arranged by subjects, places and persons. The news stories, editorials, photographs and summary articles on the events at Kent State University beginning just prior to the shooting of four students by National Guardsmen on May 4, 1970 up to a year later are available on microfilm from Bell & Howell. Everything on the film is a newsclip from the *Beacon Journal,* set up in newspaper size by the reference staff of the paper itself. Arranged chronologically, there are 164 pages preceded by an 8-page table of contents.

The idea of the microfilm is an attractive one. There is every evidence that everything run in the paper on this subject is included, but one can never be certain. The film record conveys how the major paper in the locality dealt with an important national event that happened in its own backyard. The journalistic flavor comes through strongly, giving the event an immediacy that is difficult to show in any of the numerous book and magazine accounts of the tragic events at Kent State in May 1970. There are, however, both intellectual and technical drawbacks that flaw this microfilm reel.

The typewritten table of contents at the beginning of the reel is not otherwise available from the film company. Its organization is chronological both for a summary of highlights and then within the 20 categories of the index proper. This works well because the reel of film itself is so small. The summary is not consistently faithful to its own references. Thus the first entry in the summary states that the disorders came after "peaceful demonstrations" over Nixon's policy on Cambodia while the first page of clippings begins with such quiet and peaceful headlines as "'Down With Nixon,' Scream 500 Rioting Kent Students," "Tear Gas Ends Disturbance at 3 A.M.," "7 Students and 7 Others Arrested," and "Guard Bayonets Halt Student March." At page 3 of the well-numbered film comes the unhappy news of "4 Dead 11 Wounded." Actually, the summary and index are quite adequate to the task, but a more faithful reference to headlines throughout is the preferred way to handle this.

If such a venture were to be attempted on a larger scale, it would be wise for the indexers to follow the standard subject list created by the *New York Times* and available in loose-leaf binders under the title of *The New York Times Thesaurus of Descriptors*.

The intellectual problems include the fact that there is little evidence that the *Akron Beacon Journal* is the best newspaper source on this subject. The film does show that the newspaper took a stiff editorial stand critical of the Ohio National Guard and that it ran solid summaries of the complex case as it developed. But it is not at all certain that this is a superior source over other papers in Ohio or the great national newspapers. The *Beacon Journal* does not, for instance, carry the full State Highway Patrol report on June 21, 1970, the full FBI report on July 23, the Scranton report on September 28 or other full documentation. The Akron paper simply isn't that kind of a newspaper of record which simply shows one of the limits of journalism for good scholarship as compared to government documents.

Finally, the news stories are stamped and marked up so that words are sometimes difficult to read. (To its very great credit, Bell & Howell says this in its advertising.) The stories are not always clearly dated. And this is only one year of a story that has continued to be important as further studies and further legal action ensue. The result is that the microfilm of the *Kent State University Disorders* is a handy source on a serious topic of enduring interest, put together by devoted hands in a sensible way, but with some drawbacks that are really quite evident on the face of it.

Book Reviews

Book reviews are a specialized source of reference material for political scientists. However, owing to their limited application and the difficulty one has in locating particular reviews quickly, they are not widely used as reference sources.

For research in political science, the *Social Sciences Index* and the *Index to Legal Periodicals* are good places to begin. The former indexes 263 journals in the social sciences, and reviews can often be found under author and subject headings. The latter contains a separate "Book Reviews" section in which references are (generally) entered alphabetically by author of the book reviewed.

Another good idea is to check specific political science journals. Often these journals will have an annual, cumulative index which will list the books that have been reviewed by that journal in a given year.

Finally, there are two sources with broader scopes to check: *Book Review Digest* and *Book Review Index*.

The *Digest* is an index to and digest of fiction and nonfiction appearing in 77 (as of June, 1974) selected periodicals and journals. "To qualify for inclusion a book must have been published and distributed in the United States. A work of nonfiction must have received two or more reviews" in the journals covered. Authors of the books reviewed are indexed and alphabetically followed by a subject and title index. *Book Review Digest* is published monthly and cumulated annually. Unfortunately, the *B.R. Digest* is of limited value to political scientists since only a few major journals are covered.

Book Review Index, on the other hand, is an author index of reviews published in over 200 periodicals. All reviews in each periodical indexed are cited. *BRI* is published monthly, every third issue cumulating the preceding two, with an annual cumulation. Several political science journals are covered, making it worth a look.

I once knew a college librarian who kept the *Book Review Digest* in his own office to short-circuit students seeking to use it to avoid doing an unrehearsed, naked, innocent book report for a class. At about the same time, David Reisman and others completed an important social science book titled *The Lonely Crowd* reporting an increased interest by Americans in being "inside dopesters" about political life. This attitude, long associated with the book publishing industry, has certainly blossomed in recent years. Thus the battle between lawyers over various passages in *The Death of a President* by William Manchester that were objected to by Jacqueline Kennedy was a well-known news story in the winter of 1965-66. The same thing happened in the instance of the Howard Hughes "hoax biography," never published by McGraw-Hill, which landed Clifford Irving in jail rather than at the book awards' banquets. We all read about authors, their books, contracts and hassles in *Parade, Time, Newsweek,* the *National Enquirer, Playboy* and in local newspapers. Not only did Bob Woodward and Carl Bernstein win a Pulitzer Prize in journalism for their Watergate stories in the *Washington Post;* their book *All the President's Men* became a best seller; Robert Redford decided to base a motion picture on it; and Woodward and Bernstein have appeared on TV's Today, Tonight and Tomorrow! Speculation on their chief news source, named "Deep Throat" by them, has been made in articles in *The Washingtonian,* the *Wall Street Journal* and other places, feeding our appetites as inside dopesters. Nor is this all. In 1904 George Bernard Shaw assured the success on Broadway of his play *Mrs. Warren's Profession* by coining and damning "comstockery" after Anthony

Comstock of the New York Society for the Suppression of Vice tried to close the play down. "Banned in Boston" was for years a sure-fire way to popularize a book. In 1974, Robert Moses assured success to *The Power Broker,* the biography of him written by Robert A. Caro, by issuing a long tirade against the author on the eve of the book's publication.

What does this all mean? I think it means that any self-respecting student must now learn about a book by (a) reading it, (b) using the *Book Review Digest* and *Book Review Index,* and (c) examining the history of the development of the book in every available source. It does not mean that one attempts this for every book in creation, but certainly books on politics deserve to be placed into the history of their times. This spirit is in opposition to the "great books" syndrome which stresses textual analysis only in the sense that careful reading of an author is the beginning of intellectual — and often political — adventure, not the whole of it.

Books and libraries contain so much received and conventional wisdom that their contents must be examined with beady eyes, examined and examined and examined. In praising the virtues of great historians like Gibbon, de Tocqueville, Marx, Michelet and Burckhardt, Professor John Clive of Harvard has cautioned against seeking the "truth" of events in their works. "Unlike poetry and music," Clive reasons, "the art of history is cumulative — this is to say its most recent practitioners tend to know more about events and problems of the past than their predecessors, however exalted." ("Majestic Histories Not by Fact Alone," *New York Times,* Aug 27, 1974, p. 31.)

With these things in mind, assignments for students to do book reports would require a mastery of text, author, surroundings and later, superseding events. Go ahead, hide the *Book Review Digest!*

Interlibrary Loan

With today's modern technology, students of public affairs need not be limited to what can be found in one particular library. Most academic libraries "pool" their resources through an interlibrary loan program vastly expanding the resources available. Under this program periodicals or books can be borrowed from another library (in cases of last resort, from the Library of Congress). Interlibrary loan can be a big boon to those without extensive library facilities. Learn about the details at your library, and take advantage of the infinite resources it can provide.

Ephemeral as it may at first seem to be, the *National Interlibrary Loan Code* of the American Library Association provides a basis for a system

LIBRARY BASICS 119

that is of the utmost importance for readers to comprehend. A central point is that libraries loan items to other libraries for the use of individuals which is to say that a library in California may lend to a library in Kansas for a reader, not directly to a Kansan. Generous examples abound. The Kennedy Presidential Library in Waltham, Massachusetts loans copies of photocopied oral histories to out-of-state libraries, for example.

Librarians of the "old school" who learned their manners in an age before plenty — plenty of scientists and social scientists, plenty of students, plenty of authors, plenty of publishers and plenty of teenagers knew how to do research — only a professor or a certified graduate student could use the interlibrary loan system. The times are changing, as seen in this report of a committee meeting on the subject at the 1974 meeting of the American Library Association:

> The National Interlibrary Loan Code has been under fire by several groups as being restrictive and/or discriminatory. The latest charge is that it is unfair to high school students and undergraduates and discriminates on the basis of age. While any action taken by the committee will have little effect on the lending policies of the major research libraries, a subcommittee was appointed under the chairmanship of Alice E. Wilcox to consider broadening the base of the code and to emphasize the positive aspects of lending rather than the generally accepted restrictions. (*Library of Congress Information Bulletin,* Aug. 9, 1974, Appendix 1, p. A-174)

So far as photocopying and royalty rights are concerned, every student of politics should know there is more than one school of thought than those who believe that there are plainly restrictive meanings in the Copyright Act of 1909. Like all Acts of Congress, the copyright code has been subject to many administrative and judicial interpretations. One significant recent finding shows that photocopying does not harm subscription sales of medical journals. Yet the library association committee mentioned above showed again in 1974 a certain deferential concern for the commercial interest of publishers as against their own readers' interest in "the right to read" as easily and freely as possible. This is a brief summary of how this was expressed:

> The committee expressed its concern regarding recent developments in the copyright field and emphasized the fact that interlibrary loans did not reduce the number of subscriptions to serial items, but rather was used when material was no longer available from the publisher. *(Ibid.)*

Political science students should get some practice early in using the interlibrary loan services of their chosen institution. Careful bibliographic work is likely to help in the early identification of needed articles or books. The experience will have the twin side advantage of seeing how well the system works while teaching a researcher patience and forebearance.

Bibliography

ABC Pol Sci; Advance Bibliography of Contents: Political Science and Government. Vol. 1, March 1969- . Santa Barbara, Calif.: ABC- Clio, 1969-   . 8 nos. per year.

American Library Directory. 1923-   . New York & London; R. R. Bowker Co. 29th ed. comp. by Helaine MacKeigan, 1974. Biennial.

American Newspapers, 1821-1936: A Union List of Files Available in the United States and Canada. Edited by Winifred Gregory under auspices of the Bibliographical Society of America. New York: H. W. Wilson Co., 1937.

American Political Science Review, The. Vol. 1, Nov. 1906-   . Pub. quarterly by The American Political Science Association.

Annual Ayer Directory of Publications. Vol. 1, 1880- . Philadelphia: Ayer Press, 1974. Annual.

Book Review Digest. Vol. 1, 1905-   . New York: H. W. Wilson Co. Monthly; annual cumulation.

Book Review Index. Vol. 1, no. 1, Jan. 1965-   . Detroit: Gale Research Co., 1965-   . Monthly, with quarterly cumulations.

Current Contents: Social and Behavioral Sciences. Phila.: Institute for Scientific Information, 1969- . Weekly.

Editorials on File. Jan. 1/15, 1970- . New York: Facts on File, Inc. Semimonthly.

Facts on File. Vol. 1, Oct./Nov., 1940. New York: Facts on File, 1940- Weekly, with annual bound volumes.

Index to Legal Periodical Literature. Vols. 1-6. Vols. 1-2 edited by Leonard A. Jones; Vols. 3-6 by Frank E. Chipman. Boston: Boston Book Co., 1888-1919. Chipman, 1924. Indianapolis: Bobbs-Merrill 1933. Los Angeles: Parker and Baird, 1939.

Index to Legal Periodicals, 1908- . Published for the American Association of Law Libraries. New York: H. W. Wilson Co., 1909- Monthly.

Index to the Times. 1957- . London: Times. Bimonthly.

International Bibliography of Political Science. 1953- . London: Tavistock; Chicago: Aldine Publishing Co. Vol. 1, 1954. Annual.

International Political Science Abstracts. Vol. 1, 1951- . London: Blackwell, 1952- . Quarterly. Prepared by the International Political Science Association in cooperation with the International Committee for Social Sciences Information and Documentation.

Janda, Kenneth, ed. *Computer Index to the American Political Science Review, Volumes 1-62: 1906-1968.* Xerox/University Microfilms, 1969.

Keesing's Contemporary Archives. Vol. 1, July 1, 1931- . London: Keesing's, 1931- . Weekly diary of world events with index continually up-to-date.

Microform Review. 1972-.Weston, Conn.: Microform Review, Inc. Quarterly.

National Observer Index. 1969- . Princeton, N.J.: Dow Jones & Co. Annual.

New Serial Titles, 1950-1970. Washington, D.C.: Library of Congress, 1973. New York: R. R. Bowker Co. A Union List of Serials Commencing Publication after December 31, 1949.

New York Times Index for the Published News. Sept. 1851-Dec. 1906; 1913- . Since 1948 semimonthly with annual cumulations.

New York Times Thesaurus of Descriptors, The. 2d ed. 2 vols. New York: New York Times Co., 1969.

Public Affairs Information Service Bulletin. Vol. 1, 1915- . New York Public Affairs Information Service, 1915- . Annual cumulations.

Readers' Guide to Periodical Literature. Vol. 1, 1900- . New York: H. W. Wilson Co., 1905- .

Social Sciences Index. Formerly *Social Sciences & Humanities Index.* Vol. 1, no. 1, June 1974- . New York: H. W. Wilson Co., 1974- . Quarterly.

Subject Index of the Christian Science Monitor. Vol. 1, Jan 1960- . Boston: Christian Science Monitor. Monthly, with semiannual and annual cumulations.

Ulrich's International Periodical Directory. 15th ed. New York: R. R. Bowker Co., 1973-1974.

Union List of Serials in Libraries of the United States and Canada. 3d ed. Edited by Edna Brown Titus. New York: H. W. Wilson Co., 1965. 5 vols.

U.S. Library of Congress. *Newspapers in Microform: United States, 1948-1972.* Wash. D.C., 1973. Companion volume, *Newspapers in Microform: Foreign Countries, 1948-1972.* Both supersede *Newspapers on Microfilm,* 6th ed., 1967.

_____. *Subject Headings Used in the Dictionary Catalogs of the Library of Congress.* 7th ed. Edited by Marguerite V. Quattlebaum. Wash., D.C., 1966.

Wall Street Journal Index. 1958- . Princeton, N.J.: Dow Jones & Co. Monthly with annual cumulations.

11. Files, Archives and Manuscripts

Richard M. Nixon has done wonders toward educating us about the nature, extent and significance of the records of an American President, possibly more typical than bizarre. It was learned in the summer of 1973 that he had directed the Secret Service to record thousands of hours of his White House conversations. The resulting tapes were later compelling evidence in impeachment proceedings and in several court cases. It was also disclosed later that year that his vice-presidential files from 1953 to 1961 had been donated in improper ways to the National Archives. The value assigned the papers by a professional appraiser, taken as an income tax deduction, was questioned by the Congressional Joint Committee on Finance and substantially disallowed by the Internal Revenue Service. Further, the backdating of the time one donation was made — in order to avoid the impact of a tax abuse reform provision formulated by Senator John Williams of Delaware — led to the conviction and jailing of a Nixon associate. On "Pardon Day," September 8, 1974, finally, it was announced by Mr. Philip Buchen, Counselor to President Ford, that a Washington attorney had negotiated with Mr. Nixon's attorney a "letter of agreement" between the resigned President and Arthur F. Sampson, Administrator of the General Services Administration, acting on behalf of the National Archives which is a bureaucratic part of GSA. The so-called Nixon-Sampson agreement provided for the prompt transfer of about 42 million "papers and other records, including tapes, retained during the Administration of former President Nixon" from Washington, D.C. to a depository near San Clemente, California. Because this agreement stated that Mr. Nixon had "all legal and equitable title to the Materials, including all literary rights," a view supported by an official opinion of Attorney General Saxbe issued at the same time, a set of challenges in the Congress and in the District Court for the District of Columbia ensued.

While the courts may make judgments about the "ownership" of Presidential papers, Congress and President Ford by enacting and signing into law the Presidential Recordings and Materials Preservation Act of 1974 (Public Law 93-526) are also beginning to work toward new policy on this subject. Title I governs the possession, security and accessibility of the Nixon tapes, providing that the Administrator of General Services retain custody of them. The Administrator is also directed to issue protective regulations governing public access to the materials while protecting other interests such as national security, individual rights to a fair trial, and returning to Mr. Nixon tapes or materials in which the public has no interest. Thus has Title I of Public Law 93-526 effectively abrogated the Nixon-Sampson agreement of September 1974 which had President Ford's blessing at the time it was drawn up. This title further acknowledges the litigation in process by providing for the expeditious judicial review to the legal and constitutional validity of the statute as well as to any action concerning "the question of title, ownership, custody, possession or control" of any tape recording or other material. Finally, Title I provides that "just compensation" be paid to Mr. Nixon in the event it is determined that the former President has been deprived of personal property.

A special "Public Documents Commission" is established by Title II of the Presidential Recordings and Materials Act. It will have 17 members appointed by the President, Vice President and Speaker of the House. The Commission will make recommendations by March 31, 1976 for the control, disposition, and preservation of records produced by or on behalf of "Federal officials." These are defined to include elected Federal officials and any officer of the legislative, executive or judicial branch of the Federal Government. The Commission is directed to make specific recommendations for legislation and for rules and procedures governing the documents of such officials. It will then be up to Congress and the other branches to determine more settled policies on the handling of files and the roles of the National Archives and the Library of Congress in implementing them.

If the Watergate break into Democratic National Headquarters, the ransacking of Dr. Fielding's office, and the successful photocopying and publishing of the Pentagon Papers are added to the events swirling about during the Nixon administration, many sorts of questions are raised about office files, about archives and manuscripts. These are such old questions just in the United States that it is unlikely many of them will be settled definitively in the short run. Serious and sustained attention must be given to the ownership, preservation, security, management, value and scholarly access to government files and archives as well as to the manuscripts of individuals and of voluntary associations.

Consider the fact that the comprehensive identity and location of manuscripts and archives in the United States is only gradually yielding results. Occasional finding aids and lists of holdings of some institutions,

Many sources document President Nixon's announcement on April 29, 1974 that he would release edited transcripts of conversations with his aides. (1) Portions of the address on videotape are available from the Vanderbilt Television News Archives; that of CBS alone from the National Archives. (2) The text of the address is in the *Weekly Compilation of Presidential Documents* for May 6, 1974, pp. 450-458. (3) The full 1308 page transcript, listed in the June 1974 *Monthly Catalog of U.S. Government Publications*. Distributed to all depository libraries, the document is entitled *Submission of Recorded Presidential Conversations to the Committee on the Judiciary of the House of Representatives by President Richard Nixon – April 30, 1974*. This was reprinted fully in the *Chicago Tribune* on May 1, over several days in other papers, and in paperback books by Dell with the *Washington Post* and by Bantam with the *New York Times*. (4) An analysis and lengthy excerpts of the transcripts are in the *Congressional Quarterly Weekly Report* for May 11, 1974, pp. 1151-1204. (5) More than 50 newspaper reactions are in *Editorials on File* for May 1-15, 1974, pp. 503-532. (6) Finally, another go-round began when the House Judiciary Committee issued its version of eight of the tapes, using its own equipment to duplicate the originals. On July 9 it issued a committee print, *Comparison of Passages from Transcripts of Eight Recorded Presidential Conversations*. Although widely publicized, this item may be located through the *Congressional Information Service* as well as in the *Monthly Catalog*.

---

yes; but it was not until the early 1950s that the Manuscript Division of the Library of Congress could boast of its "registers" as solid guides to particular collections. In 1961 the National Historical Publications Commission sponsored publication of the *Guide to Archives and Manuscripts in the United States,* edited by Philip M. Hamer, in one volume. Its value has led to plans for a second edition sometime later in this decade. About the same time, the Library of Congress began issuing annually volumes of a *National Union Catalog of Manuscript Collections.*

The multi-volumed *National Union Catalog of Manuscript Collections (NUCMC)* is needed for "deep" research. There are many single-volume guides to special collections, including a new one to the National Archives. The Hamer guide is comprehensive, curt and organized by states and localities.

It is difficult to believe that there has been a National Archives as such only since 1934. Created by an Act of Congress signed by President Hoover in 1930, the first great building was opened during the Roosevelt administration. Wave upon wave of new problems have faced the National Archives as it has been inundated with ever more records, old and new, and with ever more types of materials to dispose of or preserve. The huge one-volume *Guide to the National Archives of the United States,* published in 1974 by the U.S. Government Printing Office, is indispensable. This is a general guide to the noncurrent records of the U.S. Government which, as of June 30, 1970, totaled nearly one million cubic feet in volume. Thus this new *Guide* is intended to supersede all earlier general summaries and "includes all official records of the U.S. Government — now legally designated as 'The National Archives of the United States' — accessioned as of June 30, 1970, regardless of where such records are located. It does not include, however, Presidential and other personal papers and historical manuscripts in the custody of Presidential libraries." (*Guide to the National Archives of the United States,* 1974, p. 5.) The records described in this guide are located in the main building on Pennsylvania Avenue, Washington, D.C. and in ten Federal Records Centers located in different regions of the country. The place to look for descriptions of the most important records accessioned recently is *Prologue: The Journal of the National Archives,* begun in January, 1969 and now issued quarterly.

The "record group" system, developed in 1944, is so important to comprehending the organization of materials within the National Archives of the United States that a full definition is worthy of attention:

> The unit of entry in this guide is the record group; i.e., a body of organizationally and functionally related records established with particular regard for the administrative history, complexity, and volume of the records and archives of an agency. A typical record group consists of the records of a bureau of some comparable unit of an executive department at the bureau level, or the records of an independent agency of somewhat comparable importance in the Government's administrative hierarchy. (*Guide,* 1974, p. 6.)

There are several modifications of the concept. Thus there are "General Records" established for most of the executive departments and several independent agencies. Again, there are "collective records groups" to bring together the records of a number of relatively small and short-lived agencies that have an administrative or functional relationship. An example of a collective record group is seen in the Records of Presidential Committees, Commissions, and Boards which is Record Group 220.

Records of predecessor agencies are frequently included in a record group. The General Records of the Department of Housing and Urban Development (Record Group 207), for example, includes records of the Central Housing Committee, even those relating to its organization, covering the years 1931-47; the records of the Division of Defense Housing Coordination, 1941-42; records of the National Housing Agency, 1942-47; and of the Housing and Home Finance Agency, 1942-65 when the Department of Housing and Urban Development was created.

Because the National Archives and Records Service is an executive agency and mostly handles records of the Executive Branch, students tend to be unaware that the other branches are also represented in its holdings. As an historical point there are records of the Continental and Confederation Congresses and the Constitutional Convention (Record Group 360), of Revolutionary War Records (Record Group 93), as well as general records of the U.S. Government under the Constitution (Record Group 11). But there are also several record groups for Congress itself and of the files of its committees. Thus there are nearly 2,000 linear feet of unpublished petitions and memorials sent to the House between 1789 and 1962 as well as 11,415 linear feet of House committee records for the same period. The Records of the Supreme Court of the United States (Record Group 267) include minutes and dockets from the beginning and records of the Office of the Marshal and of the Clerk's Office. Teachers, researchers and students of the Supreme Court will be pleased to know that starting with the October 1955 Term, tape recordings of oral arguments before the Court have been made and these are held in Record Group 267 in the National Archives. Transcriptions of arguments in any case that was argued three or more years in the past may be obtained by seeking permission from the Marshal of the Supreme Court. These are then prepared and provided by the Audiovisual Archives Division of the National Archives for a modest fee of, say, $13.50 for the tape of an argument running an hour.

In addition to voluminous government records, some of which are maps, photographs, motion pictures, computer tapes, recordings, medals and other awards and gifts, the National Archives is authorized to accept donations from private individuals and organizations. In this category is the Ford Film Collection, motion pictures made commercially by Henry Ford early in the century. A separate catalog describes in detail this unique group of films. Enormous footage from Paramount and Pathe newsreels are also now owned by the National Archives. This film record of news exhibited to the public for half a century led the Archives in 1974 to begin accepting from the Columbia Broadcasting System video and film records

ARCHIVES 129

of the CBS Evening News and some other public interest programs. Written transcripts of each program will also be provided the National Archives by CBS.

Policy questions about archival practice and the reach of this great governmental agency are raised in many phases of its work. Thus its agreement to accession the CBS Evening News programs appeared to aid the position of the Columbia Broadcasting System in its efforts to enjoin the practices of Vanderbilt University in recording and indexing network news broadcasts through the University's Television News Archives begun in 1968. Through its six Presidential Libraries, which make up approximately one-half of the total budget of the National Archives establishment, there has often been a kind of competition for manuscripts and other materials against institutions in the private sector or at the state governmental level. Thus have the economists Seymour Harris, John Kenneth Galbraith, Walter Heller and Paul Samuelson agreed to give their lifetime papers to the Kennedy Presidential Library whereas numerous other repositories would have welcomed them. Dean Acheson decided, too, that all of his papers would go to the Truman Presidential Library while most of those of John Foster Dulles were donated to the Eisenhower Presidential Library.

The development of Presidential libraries since 1938 has accompanied the vast institutional changes in the character of the Presidential office in recent decades. President Franklin D. Roosevelt conceived of a library his friends would build on his family property in Hyde Park, New York where he would work in retirement. He attended one of the early meetings at the National Archives of the committee planning this first venture. Ad hoc planning became formalized through enactment of the Presidential Libraries Act of 1955, and since then Herbert Hoover and Harry Truman as well as Eisenhower, Kennedy and Johnson have taken advantage of its terms. The rising volume of papers in each new administration, the generous terms of the Act under which the National Archives and the National Park Service would maintain these libraries, associated museums and grounds in perpetuity, and the bountiful appropriations Congress made to back this up led the men themselves and their families to cooperate fully in donating presidential and other materials of historic interest to these six institutions. Underlying the statutory requirements were assumptions that Presidents would gladly give up papers, and the government, representing the people of the United States, would gladly care for them.

Easygoing views of these subjects were put to the test in controversies over handling materials of the last three Presidencies. The Kennedy library would be the first to attempt location in an urban center, heavily populated and congested with traffic, in Cambridge, Massachusetts near Harvard Square. Simply clearing the land took a decade by which time the environmental sensitivity of the local public and inflated building costs have repeatedly put the entire project into question. Meanwhile the Kennedy materials have been housed in the crowded and unsatisfactory Federal Records Center where fewer than ten serious researchers can be adequately serviced at a given time. In contrast, Lyndon B. Johnson and Mrs. Johnson exuberantly accepted the generosity of the Regents of the University of Texas in providing land and a building in Austin, at the University of Texas, which was an extravagant monument to a troubled administration. Indeed, Johnson's tax deductions for donating his own papers to the Library aroused Senator Williams and the rest of Congress to change the Internal Revenue Code, effective July 29, 1969, to forestall deductions for gifts of papers that were self-generated. This helped set the stage, in part, for the excesses of Richard M. Nixon, his tax troubles in the form of the backdated deed of gift and grand appraisal of vice-presidential papers and, a month after "Resignation day," of the Nixon-Sampson agreement. That agreement has been challenged both in Congress and in the Federal courts for it raised questions never before addressed in a concerted way over who, indeed, does own Presidential materials.

Meanwhile, as the importance of the Presidency had grown and as the size of all parts of the Federal government had likewise grown, a web of law was building that regulated the control of and access to government files. The Administrative Procedure Act of 1946, the Federal Records Act of 1950, the Presidential Libraries Act of 1955 and, finally, the Freedom of Information Act of 1967 and later revisions, along with numerous administrative regulations and agreements, set standard review procedures for the disposition of records. They also provided for making information in the files of government agencies — both before and after their removal to the National Archives — available to the public. True, specific categories of files were exempted from public disclosure, but the primary purpose of the Freedom of Information Act was to make information maintained by the executive branch of the Federal Government more available to the public. The high significance attached to the Freedom of Information Act is shown by its regular publication, after the Constitution, in each year's *U.S. Government Manual.*

That there has been a growth of historical and, indeed, archival interest in the country is attested to by the manner in which Congress provided for the papers of early Presidents that found their way into the Manuscript Division of the Library of Congress. Although the Library of Congress was

These published indexes are among guides to the papers of 23 American Presidents located in the Manuscript Division of the Library of Congress. The papers themselves have been microfilmed and other libraries may purchase all or part of the series, or may borrow particular reels for readers through the interlibrary loan service.

established in 1800, its development as a great national library began only a century later under the leadership of Herbert Putnam who served as Librarian of Congress from 1899 to 1939. There were fitful efforts to acquire manuscripts, Presidential and others, but even President William Howard Taft was not approached about placing his papers in the Library of Congress until some years after leaving the White House. True, by 1900 there was an established Manuscript Division and by the 1930s major collections of the papers of twenty-three Presidents were in hand. During World War II, out of fear of the possible enemy bombing of Washington, these papers were moved to more secure places — to Charlottesville, Virginia and Fort Knox, Kentucky, among other places. In 1957 Congress authorized an indexing and microfilming program for these Presidential papers that set new standards of care for such documents. The index series is alphabetized by computer and printed as registers to each collection. The papers themselves are microfilmed and have been purchased in their entirety by numerous university libraries around the country. While each index may be purchased for only a few dollars — with some exceptions for the larger ones — the entire microfilm edition of papers costs close to $20,000. Fortunately, reels may be obtained through interlibrary loan so that an impecunious student at a small college may, by examining the indexes closely in advance, order microfilm reels for research into the papers of most Presidents between Washington and Coolidge.

Politicians and other movers-and-shakers in American society today are much given to boasting that they make their important moves through personal contact, over the telephone or with cues that would mystify an experienced Parke-Bernet auctioneer. By these accounts, manuscripts in our time are small in number and of dubious value to the naive historians and social scientists who, fools that they are in the world's ways, spin theories of behavior from questionable sources of information. There is every evidence, however, that these beliefs are themselves embedded in ignorance about the character of manuscript holdings today. The Hamer *Guide to Manuscripts and Archives in the United States* provides an astonishing state-by-state, city-by-city representation of the vast and precious holdings of countless politicians, novelists, military leaders, scientists, college presidents, scholars, publishers, actors and reformers. The cumulation kept by the editors of the *National Union Catalog of Manuscript Collections* reveals that at the end of 1972 these volumes had registered some 26,000 collections located in nearly 1,000 separate repositories in the country.

Anyone conversant with even small organizations like colleges knows that both administrators and faculty have numerous file drawers, frequently enlarged and rarely emptied. The Society of American Archivists, formed in 1938, is showing rapid growth. Most states are imitating the national government by establishing or bolstering archival programs. The voluntary associations that political scientists have followed with avid interest are increasingly preserving their papers for scholarly study. The Anti-Saloon League papers are in the Michigan Historical Collections, those of the American Civil Liberties Union at Princeton, of the NAACP in the Library of Congress, the Democratic and Republican National Committees divided among Presidential Libraries.

The papers of such organizations and of individuals in public life are remarkably revealing although it has been forever true that many persons take care to sanitize their files. The opposite suspicion that an individual may have written communications "for history" is also well-founded on occasion. But the normal practice appears that when the telephone was used, notes were kept. The papers of many persons show, moreover, that they did not necessarily do their most important business by phone. The papers of Arthur T. Vanderbilt, a President of the American Bar Association, leader of New York University Law School, founder of the Citizenship Clearing House and Chief Justice of New Jersey, which are now open for study in the Collection on Legal Change at Wesleyan University, include a vast correspondence full of frank exchange as well as docket books of judicial decision-making that is most revealing. The papers of other jurists such as those of Jerome Frank at Yale, of Frank Murphy at Michigan, and Felix Frankfurter, Harold Burton, Harlan Stone and others in the Library of Congress are replete with recitations of intimate, inside stories.

Oral history came in with the tape recorder in the late 1940s when the redoubtable historian Allan Nevins led the establishment of a special program at Columbia University to arrange for people in many fields to reminisce for posterity. Special projects such as the early development of radio and of advertising, the New Deal and New York City politics were chosen for emphasis. Gradually, through the transcription of interviews and their checking by the respondent, Columbia has built an unprecedented addition to its already great manuscript collections in Butler Library. Columbia has issued a one-volume catalog to its collection of oral histories and this work has been widely copied, receiving sufficient respectability to be included in listings in the *National Union Catalog of Manuscript Collections.*

Still another form that manuscripts are taking today is through the editing of letterpress editions of the papers of notable national figures through a program established by the National Historical Publications

Commission, a part of the National Archives and Records Service in Washington. Instead of searching around the country for occasional papers on a subject, it is possible through this program to consult the numerous correspondence and other papers of such figures as Washington, the Adams family, Jefferson, Jackson and Lincoln by reading books that faithfully reproduce their original manuscripts. The program has been branching out in recent years and other institutions in addition to NHPC have entered the picture. Thus there are projects to publish, in part often times, the papers of Frederick Douglass, Booker T. Washington and W. E. B. DuBois.

In raising the consciousness of political scientists about government files (which they may seek to examine through the routines of the Freedom of Information Act), about archives and manuscripts, I do not hope to convert the unwashed to become historians. On the contrary, it appears frequently that political scientists will find in original records more faithful data than are available in the reference books and libraries discussed elsewhere in these pages. Archives and manuscripts are no longer arcane sources out of the reach of both undergraduate and graduate students of political science. By tapping these exciting sources all political scientists will be able to supplement established research routines.

Bibliography

Hamer, Philip M., ed. *Guide to Archives and Manuscripts in the United States.* New Haven: Yale University Press, 1961.

U.S., Library of Congress. *National Union Catalog of Manuscript Collections.* 1972 and Index 1970-1972, vol. 11. Washington, D.C., 1974. Vol. 1, 1959-61. Ann Arbor, Mich.: J. W. Edwards, 1962. Vol. 2, 1962 and Index 1959-1962, 2 vols. Hamden, Conn.: Shoe String Press, 1964. Thereafter by Library of Congress.

U.S., National Archives. *Guide to the National Archives of the United States.* Washington, D.C.: National Archives and Records Service, General Services Administration, 1974.

U.S., National Archives. *Prologue: The Journal of the National Archives.* Vol. 1, no. 1, Jan. 1969- . Washington, D.C.: National Archives Trust Fund. Quarterly, since 1972.

Ref
Z
7165
U5
V67